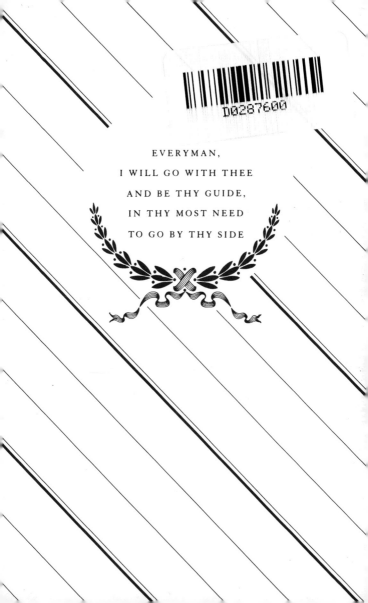

EVERYMAN,
I WILL GO WITH THEE
AND BE THY GUIDE,
IN THY MOST NEED
TO GO BY THY SIDE

EVERYMAN'S LIBRARY
POCKET POETS

Prayers

Selected and edited by
Peter Washington

EVERYMAN'S LIBRARY

POCKET POETS

Alfred A. Knopf · New York · Toronto

THIS IS A BORZOI BOOK

PUBLISHED BY ALFRED A. KNOPF, INC.

This selection by Peter Washington first published in
Everyman's Library, 1995
Copyright © 1995 by David Campbell Publishers Ltd.

A list of acknowledgments to copyright holders can be found at the back
of this volume.

ISBN 0-679-44466-1

Typography by Peter B. Willberg

Typeset in the UK by Acc Computing, Queen Camel, Somerset

Printed and bound in Germany by
Mohndruck Graphische Betriebe GmbH, Gütersloh

CONTENTS

Foreword   13

MATINS

GEORGE HERBERT Prayer   17
JULIAN OF NORWICH Meditation   18
EMILY DICKINSON Prayer is the little implement.. ..   18
From THE CLOUD OF UNKNOWING Private Prayers ..   19
GEORGE HERBERT How should I praise thee, Lord!..   24
HEINRICH SUSO Meditation..   26
CHRISTOPHER SMART Adoration   27
SIMONE WEIL Repeating the Name   28
MADAME GUYON The Method of Prayer   29
ST JOHN OF THE CROSS Verses Written after an
    Ecstasy of High Exaltation   32
THOMAS TRAHERNE On the Bible   35
C. S. LEWIS *From* Chiefly on Prayer   36
JOHN DONNE Inattentive Prayer..   38
EMILY DICKINSON There comes an hour when
    begging stops   39
WILLIAM COWPER Exhortation to Prayer   40
ST ANSELM Lord, teach me to seek Thee   42
EMILY DICKINSON My period had come for Prayer ..   43
JOHN HENRY NEWMAN Praise to the Holiest in the
    height   44
JOHN DONNE Prayer   46

GEORGE HERBERT Jordan (1)   48
               Jordan (2)   49
WILLIAM BLAKE The Divine Image   50
THOMAS TRAHERNE *From* The Fourth Century   51
SIMONE WEIL On Prayer   54
GEORGE HERBERT Love   56

PRIME
THOMAS KEN Awake, My Soul   59
FRANCIS KILVERT *From* the Diary, 11 July, 1870 ..   61
GERARD MANLEY HOPKINS Pied Beauty   63
DIETRICH BONHOEFFER O God, early in the morning
      I cry to you   64
JOHN KEBLE Morning Hymn   65
CHRISTINA ROSSETTI God strengthen me   66
RANDALL JARRELL A Prayer at Morning   67
CHARLES WESLEY Forth in thy name, O Lord, I go ..   68
W. H. AUDEN Prime   69
From THE BHAGAVAD–GĪTĀ Lord of fire and death ..   71
From THE SERVICE OF THE ORTHODOX SYNAGOGUE
      Jewish Prayer   72
From THE DEAD SEA SCROLLS Great and holy is the
      Lord   73
GEORGE GASCOIGNE Gascoigne's Good-morrow   ..   74
FRANCIS QUARLES The Divine Lover   78
AL-ANSARI O Lord, in Mercy grant my soul to live   80
From THE KORAN   80

TIERCE

JOHN BUNYAN The Pilgrim Song 83

JOHN MILTON On His Blindness 84

ANON. Arabic Prayer 84

JOHN DRINKWATER The Deed 85

ST IGNATIUS LOYOLA Obedience 87

MOTHER TERESA Prayer 87

WILLIAM LANGLAND For the Poor 88

ST FRANCIS OF ASSISI Lord, make me an instrument
of Thy peace 90

SENGTS'AN On Trust in the Heart 91

WILLIAM LANGLAND Charity's Child 92

JOSEPHINE DELPHINE HENDERSON HEARD Doxology . . 93

A. H. CLOUGH The Latest Decalogue 94

ROBERT HERRICK His Creed 95

TEILHARD DE CHARDIN Hymn to Matter 96

GERARD MANLEY HOPKINS God's Grandeur 97

C. S. LEWIS Thy Kingdom Come 98

ST ANSELM Let me seek you by desiring you 100

ST FRANCIS OF ASSISI Cantica 101

CHARLES WESLEY O thou who camest from above . . 102

THOMAS À KEMPIS Grant to me, O Lord 103

BERAKOTH Close mine eyes from evil 103

SIMONE WEIL *From* Waiting on God 104

CHRISTOPHER SMART Long-suffering of God 107

WILLIAM COWPER Light Shining out of Darkness . . 108

TUKARAM Six Prayers from an Indian Peasant 110

WILLIAM WORDSWORTH Resolution and
Independence 115
SIR FRANCIS DRAKE Prayer before Cadiz 122
WINIFRED HOLTBY Epitaph 122

SEXT
THOMAS TRAHERNE *From* The Third Century 125
HENRY VAUGHAN The Retreat 127
GERARD MANLEY HOPKINS As kingfishers catch fire 129
The Windhover 130
ST FRANCIS OF ASSISI O most high, almighty, good
Lord God 131
From CHANDOGYA UPANISHAD Brahman 133
PERCY BYSSHE SHELLEY Song of Apollo 134
BARNABE BARNES God's Virtue 136
TEILHARD DE CHARDIN Lord, enfold me 137
ANN GRIFFITHS Wonderful to come out living 137
SIR PHILIP SIDNEY Splendidis Longum Valedico
Nugis 138
JOHN DRYDEN Veni Creator Spiritus 139
ST HILDEGARDE Fire of the Spirit 141
GERARD MANLEY HOPKINS My prayers must meet a
brazen heaven 142
J. BYROM My spirit longs for Thee 143
ABU HAMID AL-GHAZALI Praise be to him who alone
is to be praised 144
HENRY VAUGHAN Ascension Hymn 145

ST FRANCIS OF ASSISI All creatures of our God and
  King 147

NONES

THOMAS TRAHERNE *From* The First Century 151
From THE CLOUD OF UNKNOWING 152
JOHN GREENLEAF WHITTIER *From* The Brewing of
  Soma 155
ROBERT HERRICK I'll hope no more 157
MADAME GUYON Of the Presence of God 158
WILLIAM DEAN HOWELLS Lord, for the erring
  thought 162
From THE SUTTA NIPĀTA The Song of Blessing .. 163
JALĀL AL-DĪN RŪMĪ Do you seek no more of Him .. 165
ALCUIN OF YORK The Will of God 167
SØREN KIERKEGAARD The Unchangeableness of God 168
GERARD MANLEY HOPKINS The Habit of Perfection .. 171
THOMAS TRAHERNE It is Good to be Happy Alone .. 173
D. M. DOLBEN I asked for Peace 176
SIR WALTER RALEGH *From* His Pilgrimage 177
GEORGE HERBERT Peace 178
From THE VEDAS May there be peace 180
ROBERT SOUTHWELL Look Home 181
HENRY VAUGHAN Peace 183
LOHAN HOSHANG OF SHŌSHU Wherever I went 184
SOCRATES Beloved Pan 185
RAMAKRISHNA There are three different paths 185

VESPERS

BUNAN The Moon 189

GETSUDO Cloud Street 189

GERARD MANLEY HOPKINS Hurrahing in Harvest .. 190

FRANCIS KILVERT *From* the Diary, 14 March,
1871 191

GERARD MANLEY HOPKINS My own heart let me
more have pity on 193

RABINDRANATH TAGORE When the heart is hard .. 194

THE KADDISH 195

From THE CLOUD OF UNKNOWING St Denis's Prayer .. 196

PETER ABELARD Vespers: Saturday Evening 197

EDMUND SPENSER *From* Amoretti 200

From THE ELIZABETHAN PRAYER BOOK Forgiveness 201

ANON. Keep Me from Sinkin' Down 202

SOLOMON IBN GABRIOL Lord of the world 203

ANON. I asked for strength 204

ALCUIN OF YORK Grace 205

ROBERT HERRICK Two Graces for Children 206

PRIMO LEVI Shemà 207

ALCUIN OF YORK When you sit happy 208

TULSI DAS Show love to all creatures 208

ANON. Have mercy on me 208

THOMAS KEN At the Door of a Christian Hospital .. 209

COMPLINE

JOHN HENRY NEWMAN Guidance 213

NECHUM BRONZE Lord, let Your light be only for
the day 214

THOMAS KEN All praise to Thee, my God, this night 215

JOHN CLARE Lord, Hear my Prayer 216

ROBERT HERRICK In the hour of my distress 218

ANNE BRADSTREET Lord, why should I doubt 219

ANON. Prayer in Darkness of Spirit 220

HENRY FRANCIS LYTE Abide with me 221

ISRAEL ABRAHAMS When all within is dark 222

ST JOHN OF THE CROSS Songs of the Soul in Rapture 223

HENRY VAUGHAN The Night 226

ALCUIN OF YORK His Epitaph 229

RAHMĀN BĀBA No matter where I turn my head .. 231

JOHN DONNE Thou hast made me 232

ROBERT HERRICK Divination by a Daffadill 233

SIR WALTER RALEGH Even such is Time 233

ISAAC WATTS Submission to Afflictive Providences 234

CHRISTINA ROSSETTI Before the Beginning 236

THOMAS CAMPION Prayer 237

JOHN DONNE Hymn to God the Father 238

ROBERT HERRICK To his Sweet Saviour 239

PRUDENTIUS Before Sleep 240

From THE UPANISHADS 241

BUDDHA Now may every living thing 241

From THE SARUM MISSAL God be in my head 242

Acknowledgments 245

Index of First Lines 249

FOREWORD

This collection of prayers and meditations is not intended as a devotional handbook, though I suppose it might be used as such. It teaches no doctrine. If the book has a purpose, one might call it, in Coleridge's phrase, a set of 'Aids to Reflection'.

The text is divided into seven sections which correspond to the seven canonical hours of the Christian church – which in turn take their cue from David's declaration in Psalm 119: 'Seven times a day do I praise thee'. Religious orders still follow this pattern of worship, though they vary the names, times and forms of the hours. Commonly the sequence begins with matins at 3am, followed by prime (6am), tierce (9am), sext (12am), nones (3pm), vespers (6pm) and compline (9pm).

The ordering of prayers for particular times of the day is by no means unique to Christianity. Many religions link their daily observances to the rhythms of nature and the human body. Though the divisions between sections in this book are not rigid, the items gathered here are therefore broadly matched to what I have perceived as the mood of the hour.

PETER WASHINGTON

*Prayer does not change God, but
it changes him who prays.*

SØREN KIERKEGAARD

MATINS

PRAYER

Prayer, the Church's banquet, Angels' age,
    God's breath in man returning to his birth,
The soul in paraphrase, heart in pilgrimage,
    The Christian plummet, sounding heaven and earth;
Engine against the Almighty, sinner's tower,
    Reversed thunder, Christ-side-piercing spear,
The six-days' world transposing in an hour,
    A kind of tune, which all things hear and fear;
Softness, and peace, and joy, and love, and bliss,
    Exalted manna, gladness of the best,
    Heaven in ordinary, man well drest,
The milky way, the bird of Paradise,
    Church-bells beyond the stars heard, the soul's
            blood,
    The land of spices; something understood.

MEDITATION

Prayer unites the soul to God. For though the soul be
ever like to God in nature and substance, restored by
grace, it is often unlike in condition by sin on man's part.
Then is prayer a witness that the soul wills as God wills,
and it comforts the conscience and enables man to
grace. And so He teaches us to pray and mightily trust
that we shall have it. For He beholdeth us in love and
would *make us partners of His good deed.* And therefore
He moves us to pray for that which it pleases Him to do.

JULIAN OF NORWICH (c. 1342–1413)

PRAYER IS THE LITTLE IMPLEMENT

Prayer is the little implement
Through which Men reach
Where Presence – is denied them.
They fling their Speech

By means of it – in God's Ear –
If then He hear –
This sums the Apparatus
Comprised in Prayer –

18   EMILY DICKINSON (1830–1886)

PRIVATE PRAYERS
From THE CLOUD OF UNKNOWING

Just as the meditations of those who seek to live the contemplative life come without warning, so, too, do their prayers. I am thinking of their private prayers, of course, not those laid down by Holy Church. For true contemplatives could not value such prayers more, and so they use them, in the form and according to the rules laid down by the holy Fathers before us. But their own personal prayers rise spontaneously to God, without bidding of premeditation, beforehand or during their prayer.

If they are in words, as they seldom are, then they are very few words; the fewer the better. If it is a little word of one syllable, I think it is better than if it is of two, and more in accordance with the work of the Spirit. For a contemplative should always live at the highest, topmost peak spiritually.

We can illustrate this by looking at nature. A man or woman, suddenly frightened by fire, or death, or what you will, is suddenly in his extremity of spirit driven hastily and by necessity to cry or pray for help. And how does he do it? Not, surely, with a spate of words; not even in a single word of two syllables! Why? He thinks it wastes too much time to declare his urgent need and his agitation. So he bursts out in his terror with one little word, and that of a single syllable: 'Fire!' it may be, or 'Help!'

Just as this little word stirs and pierces the ears of the hearers more quickly, so too does a little word of one syllable, when it is not merely spoken or thought, but expresses also the intention in the depth of our spirit. Which is the same as the 'height' of our spirit, for in these matters height, depth, length, and breadth all mean the same. And it pierces the ears of Almighty God more quickly than any long psalm churned out unthinkingly. That is why it is written 'Short prayer penetrates heaven.'

Why does it penetrate heaven, this short little prayer of one syllable? Surely because it is prayed with a full heart, in the height and depth and length and breadth of the spirit of him that prays it. In the height, for it is with all the might of his spirit; in the depth, for in this little syllable is contained all that the spirit knows; in the length, for should it always feel as it does now, it would always cry to God as it now cries; in the breadth, for it would extend to all men what it wills for itself.

At this time the soul understands what St Paul and all saints speak of – not fully, perhaps, but as much as one can at this stage of contemplation – and that is, what is the length and breadth and height and depth of the everlasting, all-loving, all-mighty, all-knowing God. God's everlastingness is his length; his love is his breadth; his might is his height; and his wisdom is his depth. No wonder that a soul moulded by grace into the close image and likeness of God his maker is so soon heard by God! Yes, even if it is a very sinful soul, who is as it were an enemy of God. If he through grace were to cry such a short syllable in the height, depth, length, and breadth of his spirit, he would always be heard because of this anguished cry, and be helped by God.

An example will show this. If you were to hear your deadly enemy in terror cry out from the depth of his being this little word 'Fire!' or 'Help!', you, without reckoning he was your enemy, out of sheer pity aroused by his despairing cry, would rise up, even on a mid-winter night, and help him put out his fire, or quieten and ease his distress. Oh Lord! since grace can make a man so merciful as to show great mercy and pity to his enemy despite his enmity, what pity and mercy shall God have for the spiritual cry of a soul that comes from its height and depth and length and breadth! God has in his nature all that man acquires by grace. And much more, incomparably more mercy will God have, since the natural endowment of a thing makes it basically more kin to eternal things than that which is given it later by grace.

We must therefore pray in the height, depth, length, and breadth of our spirits. Not in many words, but in a little word of one syllable. What shall this word be?

Surely such a word as is suited to the nature of prayer itself. And what word is that? First let us see what prayer is in itself, and then we shall know more clearly what word will best suit its nature.

In itself prayer is nothing else than a devout setting of our will in the direction of God in order to get good, and remove evil. Since all evil is summed up in sin, considered causally or essentially, when we pray with intention for the removing of evil, we should neither say, think, nor mean any more than this little word 'sin'. And if we pray with intention for the acquiring of goodness, let us pray, in word or thought or desire, no other word than 'God'. For in God is all good, for he is its beginning and its being. Do not be surprised then that I set these words before all others. If I could find any shorter words which would sum up fully the thought of good or evil as these words do, or if I had been led by God to take some other words, then I would have used those and left these. And that is my advice for you too.

But don't study these words, for you will never achieve your object so, or come to contemplation; it is never attained by study, but only by grace. Take no other words for your prayer, despite all I have said, than those that God leads you to use. Yet if God does lead you to these, my advice is not to let them go, that is, if you are using words at all in your prayer: not otherwise.

They are very short words. But though shortness of prayer is greatly to be recommended here, it does not mean that the frequency of prayer is to be lessened. For as I have said, it is prayed in the length of one's spirit, so that it never stops until such time as it has fully attained what it longs for. We can turn to our terrified man or woman for an example. They never stop crying their little words 'Help!' or 'Fire!' till such time as they have got all the help they need in their trouble.

HOW SHOULD I PRAISE THEE, LORD!

How should I praise thee, Lord! how should my rymes
    Gladly engrave thy love in steel,
    If what my soul doth feel sometimes,
       My soul might ever feel!

Although there were some fourtie heav'ns, or more,
    Sometimes I peere above them all;
    Sometimes I hardly reach a score,
       Sometimes to hell I fall.

O rack me not to such a vast extent;
    Those distances belong to thee:
    The world's too little for thy tent,
       A grave too big for me.

Wilt thou meet arms with man, that thou dost stretch
    A crumme of dust from heav'n to hell?
    Will great God measure with a wretch?
       Shall he thy stature spell?

O let me, when thy roof my soul hath hid,
    O let me roost and nestle there:
    Then of a sinner thou art rid,
       And I of hope and fear.

Yet take thy way; for sure thy way is best:
    Stretch or contract me thy poore debter:
    This is but tuning of my breast,
        To make the musick better.

Whether I flie with angels, fall with dust,
    Thy hands made both, and I am there:
    Thy power and love, my love and trust
        Make one place ev'ry where.

MEDITATION

I place before my inward eyes myself with all that I am –
my body, soul, and all my powers – and I gather round
me all the creatures which God ever created in heaven,
on earth, and in all the elements, each one severally with
its name, whether birds of the air, beasts of the forest,
fishes of the water, leaves and grass of the earth, or the
innumerable sand of the sea, and to these I add all the
little specks of dust which glance in the sunbeams, with
all the little drops of water which ever fell or are falling
from dew, snow, or rain, and I wish that each of these
had a sweetly sounding stringed instrument, fashioned
from my heart's inmost blood, striking on which they
might each send up to our dear and gentle God a new
and lofty strain of praise for ever and ever. And then the
loving arms of my soul stretch out and extend themselves towards the innumerable multitude of all creatures, and my intention is, just as a free and blithesome
leader of a choir stirs up the singers of his company,
even so to turn them all to good account by inciting
them to sing joyously, and to offer up their hearts to
God. 'Sursum corda.'

26   HEINRICH SUSO (*c.* 1300–1366),
       TRANS. T. F. KNOX

ADORATION

For ADORATION seasons change,
And order, truth, and beauty range,
   Adjust, attract, and fill:
The grass the polyanthus cheques;
And polish'd porphyry reflects,
   By the descending rill.

Rich almonds colour to the prime
For ADORATION; tendrils climb,
   And fruit-trees pledge their gems;
And Ivis, with her gorgeous vest,
Builds for her eggs her cunning nest,
   And bell-flowers bow their stems.

Now labour his reward receives,
For ADORATION counts his sheaves,
   To peace, her bounteous prince;
The nectarine his strong tint imbibes,
And apples of ten thousand tribes,
   And quick peculiar quince.

REPEATING THE NAME

The whole virtue of religious practices can be conceived of from the Buddhist tradition concerning the recitation of the name of the Lord. It is said that Buddha made a vow to raise to himself, in the Land of Purity, all those who pronounced his name with the desire of being saved by him; and that because of this vow the recitation of the name of the Lord really has the power of transforming the soul.

Religion is nothing else but this promise of God. Every religious practice, every rite, all liturgy is a form of the recitation of the name of the Lord and in principle should have a real virtue, the virtue of saving whoever devotes himself to performing it with desire.

All religions pronounce the name of God in their particular language. As a rule it is better for a man to name God in his native tongue rather than in one that is foreign to him. Except in special cases the soul is not able to abandon itself utterly when it has to make the slight effort of seeking for the words in a foreign language, even when this language is well known.

SIMONE WEIL (1909–1943),
    TRANS. EMMA CRAUFURD

THE METHOD OF PRAYER

There are two ways of introducing a soul into prayer, which should for some time be pursued; the one is Meditation, the other is Reading accompanied with Meditation.

Meditative Reading is the choosing some important practical or speculative truth, always preferring the practical, and proceeding thus: whatever truth you have chosen, read only a small portion of it, endeavouring to taste and digest it, to extract the essence and substance thereof, and proceed no farther while any savour or relish remains in the passage: when this subsides, take up your book again and proceed as before, seldom reading more than half a page at a time; for it is not the quantity that is read, but the manner of reading, that yields us profit.

Those who read fast reap no more advantage than a bee would by only skimming over the surface of the flower, instead of waiting to penetrate into it, and extract its sweets. Much reading is rather for scholastic subjects than divine truths: indeed, to receive real profit from spiritual books, we must read as I have described; and I am certain, if that method were pursued, we should become gradually habituated to, and more fully disposed for prayer.

Meditation, which is the other method, is to be

practised at an appropriated season, and not in the time of reading. I believe the best manner of meditating is as follows: – When, by an act of lively faith, you are placed in the Presence of GOD, recollect some truth wherein there is substance and food; pause gently and sweetly thereon, not to employ the reason, but merely to calm and fix the mind: for you must observe, that your principal exercise should ever be the Presence of GOD; your subject, therefore, should rather serve to stay the mind, than exercise the understanding.

From this procedure, it will necessarily follow, that the lively faith in a GOD immediately present in our inmost soul, will produce an eager and vehement pressing inwardly into ourselves, and a restraining all our senses from wandering abroad: this serves to extricate us speedily from numberless distractions, to remove us far from external objects, and to bring us nigh unto our GOD, Who is only to be found in our inmost centre, which is the Holy of Holies wherein He dwelleth.

He hath even promised *'to come and make his abode with him that doth his will'* (John xiv. 23). S. Augustine accuses himself of wasting his time, by not having from the first sought GOD in this manner of prayer.

When we are thus fully introverted, and warmly penetrated throughout with a living sense of the Divine Presence; when the senses are all recollected, and withdrawn from the circumference to the centre, and the soul is sweetly and silently employed on the truths we have read, not in reasoning, but in feeding thereon, and in animating the will by affection, rather than fatiguing the understanding by study; when, I say, the affections are in this state, which, however difficult it may appear at first, is, as I shall hereafter show, easily attainable; we must allow them sweetly to repose, and peacefully to drink in that of which they have tasted: for as a person may enjoy the flavour of the finest viand in mastication, yet receive no nourishment therefrom, if he does not cease the action and swallow the food; so, when our affections are enkindled, if we endeavour to stir them up yet more, we extinguish their flame, and the soul is deprived of its nourishment; we should, there-fore, in stillness and repose, with respect, confidence and love, swallow the blessed food of which we have tasted: this method is, indeed, highly necessary; and will advance the soul farther in a short time, than any other in a course of years.

MADAME GUYON (1648–1717),
TRANS. ANON.

VERSES WRITTEN AFTER AN ECSTASY OF HIGH EXALTATION

I entered in, I know not where,
And I remained, though knowing naught,
Transcending knowledge with my thought.

Of when I entered I know naught,
But when I saw that I was there
(Though where it was I did not care)
Strange things I learned, with greatness fraught.
Yet what I heard I'll not declare.
But there I stayed, though knowing naught,
Transcending knowledge with my thought.

Of peace and piety interwound
This perfect science had been wrought,
Within the solitude profound
A straight and narrow path it taught,
Such secret wisdom there I found
That there I stammered, saying naught,
But topped all knowledge with my thought.

So borne aloft, so drunken-reeling,
So rapt was I, so swept away,
Within the scope of sense or feeling
My sense or feeling could not stay.
And in my soul I felt, revealing,
A sense that, though its sense was naught,
Transcended knowledge with my thought.

The man who truly there has come
Of his own self must shed the guise;
Of all he knew before the sum
Seems far beneath that wondrous prize:
And in this lore he grows so wise
That he remains, though knowing naught,
Transcending knowledge with his thought.

The farther that I climbed the height
The less I seemed to understand
The cloud so tenebrous and grand
That there illuminates the night.
For he who understands that sight
Remains for aye, though knowing naught,
Transcending knowledge with his thought.

This wisdom without understanding
Is of so absolute a force
No wise man of whatever standing
Can ever stand against its course,
Unless they tap its wondrous source,
To know so much, though knowing naught,
They pass all knowledge with their thought.

This summit all so steeply towers
And is of excellence so high
No human faculties or powers
Can ever to the top come nigh.
Whoever with its steep could vie,
Though knowing nothing, would transcend
All thought, forever, without end.

If you would ask, what is its essence –
This summit of all sense and knowing:
It comes from the Divinest Presence –
The sudden sense of Him outflowing,
In His great clemency bestowing
The gift that leaves men knowing naught,
Yet passing knowledge with their thought.

34   ST JOHN OF THE CROSS (1542–1591),
       TRANS. ROY CAMPBELL

ON THE BIBLE

When Thou dost take
   this sacred Book into thy hand;
Think not that Thou
   th' included sence dost understand.

It is a signe
   thou wantest sound Intelligence;
If that Thou think
   thy selfe to understand the Sence.

Bee not deceived
   Thou then on it in vain mayst gaze
The way is intricate
   that leads into a Maze.

Heer's nought but whats Mysterious
   to an Understanding Eye:
Where Reverence alone stands Ope,
   And Sence stands By.

From CHIEFLY ON PRAYER

And you may well say 'act'. For what I call 'myself' (for
all practical, everyday purposes) is also a dramatic
construction; memories, glimpses in the shaving-glass,
and snatches of the very fallible activity called 'intro-
spection', are the principal ingredients. Normally I call
this construction 'me', and the stage set 'the real world.'

Now the moment of prayer is for me – or involves for
me as its condition – the awareness, the reawakened
awareness, that this 'real world' and 'real self' are very
far from being rock-bottom realities. I cannot, in the
flesh, leave the stage, either to go behind the scenes or
to take my seat in the pit; but I can remember that these
regions exist. And I also remember that my apparent
self – this clown or hero or super – under his grease-
paint is a real person with an off-stage life. The dramatic
person could not tread the stage unless he concealed a
real person: unless the real and unknown I existed, I
would not even make mistakes about the imagined me.
And in prayer this real I struggles to speak, for once,
from his real being, and to address, for once, not the
other actors, but – what shall I call Him? The Author,
for He invented us all? The Producer, for He controls
all? Or the Audience, for He watches, and will judge, the
performance?

The attempt is not to escape from space and time and from my creaturely situation as a subject facing objects. It is more modest: to re-awake the awareness of that situation. If that can be done, there is no need to go anywhere else. This situation itself, is, at every moment, a possible theophany. Here is the holy ground; the Bush is burning now.

Of course this attempt may be attended with almost every degree of success or failure. The prayer preceding all prayers is, 'May it be the real I who speaks. May it be the real Thou that I speak to.' Infinitely various are the levels from which we pray. Emotional intensity is in itself no proof of spiritual depth. If we pray in terror we shall pray earnestly; it only proves that terror is an earnest emotion. Only God Himself can let the bucket down to the depths in us. And, on the other side, He must constantly work as the iconoclast. Every idea of Him we form, He must in mercy shatter. The most blessed result of prayer would be to rise thinking, 'But I never knew before. I never dreamed . . .' I suppose it was at such a moment that Thomas Aquinas said of all his own theology: 'It reminds me of straw.'

INATTENTIVE PRAYER

If at any time having cast thyself into the posture of prayer, upon thy knees, and entered into thy prayer, thou have found thyself withdrawn, transported, strayed into some deviations, and by-thoughts; Thou must not think all that devotion lost; much less, that prayer to be turned into sin; for God, who hath put all thy tears into his bottle, all thy words into his register, all thy sighs into his bosom, will also spread that zeal with which thou enteredst into thy prayer, over thy whole prayer, and where that (thine own zeal) is too short, Christ Jesus himself will spread his prayer over thine, and say, Give him, O Father, that which he hath asked faithfully in my name, and, where he hath fallen into any deviations or negligences, Father forgive him, though he knew not what he said.

THERE COMES AN HOUR WHEN BEGGING STOPS

There comes an hour when begging stops,
When the long interceding lips
Perceive their prayer is vain.
'Thou shalt not' is a kinder sword
Than from a disappointing God
'Disciple, call again.'

EXHORTATION TO PRAYER

What various hindrances we meet
In coming to a mercy-seat!
Yet who that knows the worth of pray'r
But wishes to be often there?

Pray'r makes the dark'ned cloud withdraw,
Pray'r climbs the ladder Jacob saw,
Gives exercise to faith and love,
Brings ev'ry blessing from above.

Restraining pray'r, we cease to fight;
Pray'r makes the Christian's armour bright;
And Satan trembles, when he sees
The weakest saint upon his knees.

While Moses stood with arms spread wide,
Success was found on Israel's side;
But when thro' weariness they fail'd,
That moment Amalek prevail'd.

Have you no words? Ah, think again!
Words flow apace when you complain
And fill your fellow-creature's ear
With the sad tale of all your care.

Were half the breath thus vainly spent
To heav'n in supplication sent,
Your cheerful song would oft'ner be:
'Hear what the Lord has done for me!'

LORD, TEACH ME TO SEEK THEE

Lord, teach me to seek Thee, and reveal Thyself to me when I seek Thee. For I cannot seek Thee except Thou teach me, nor find Thee except Thou reveal Thyself. Let me seek Thee in longing, let me long for Thee in seeking: let me find Thee in love and love Thee in finding. Lord, I acknowledge and I thank Thee that Thou hast created me in this Thine image, in order that I may be mindful of Thee and love Thee: but that image has been so consumed and wasted away by vices and obscured by the smoke of wrong-doing that it cannot achieve that for which it was made, except Thou renew it and create it anew. Is the eye of the soul darkened by its infirmity, or dazzled by Thy glory? Surely, it is both darkened in itself and dazzled by Thee. Lord, this is the unapproachable light in which Thou dwellest. Truly I see it not, because it is too bright for me; and yet whatever I see, I see through it, as the weak eye sees what it sees through the light of the sun, which in the sun itself it cannot look upon. Oh supreme and unapproachable light, oh holy and blessed truth, how far art Thou from me who am so near to Thee, how far art Thou removed from my vision, though I am so near to Thine! Everywhere Thou art wholly present, and I see Thee not. In Thee I move and in Thee I have my being, and cannot come to Thee; Thou art within me and about me, and I feel Thee not.

ST ANSELM (1033?–1109),
TRANS. BENEDICTA WARD

MY PERIOD HAD COME FOR PRAYER

My period had come for Prayer –
No other Art – would do –
My Tactics missed a rudiment –
Creator – Was it you?

God grows above – so those who pray
Horizons – must ascend –
And so I stepped upon the North
To see this Curious Friend –

His House was not – no sign had He –
By Chimney – nor by Door
Could I infer his Residence –
Vast Prairies of Air

Unbroken by a Settler –
Were all that I could see –
Infinitude – Had'st Thou no Face
That I might look on Thee?

The Silence condescended –
Creation stopped – for Me –
But awed beyond my errand –
I worshipped – did not 'pray' –

EMILY DICKINSON (1830–1886)

PRAISE TO THE HOLIEST IN THE HEIGHT

Praise to the Holiest in the height,
   And in the depth be praise;
In all his words most wonderful,
   Most sure in all his ways.

O loving wisdom of our God!
   When all was sin and shame,
A second Adam to the fight
   And to the rescue came.

O wisest love! that flesh and blood,
   Which did in Adam fail,
Should strive afresh against the foe,
   Should strive and should prevail;

And that a higher gift than grace
   Should flesh and blood refine,
God's presence and his very self,
   And essence all-divine.

O generous love! that he who smote
    In Man, for man, the foe,
The double agony in Man,
    For man, should undergo;

And in the garden secretly,
    And on the cross on high,
Should teach his brethren, and inspire
    To suffer and to die.

Praise to the Holiest in the height,
    And in the depth be praise;
In all his words most wonderful,
    Most sure in all his ways.

PRAYER

The Church is the house of prayer, so, as that upon occasion, preaching may be left out, but never a house of preaching, so, as that prayer may be left out. And for the debt of prayer, God will not be paid, with money of our own coining, (with sudden, extemporal, inconsiderate prayer) but with current money, that bears the King's image, and inscription; The Church of God, by his ordinance, hath set his stamp, upon a liturgy and service, for his house. *Audit Deus in corde cogitantis, quod nec ipse audit, qui cogitat,* says St Bernard: God hears the very first motions of a man's heart, which, that man, till he proceed to a farther consideration, doth not hear, not feel, not deprehend in himself.

That soul, that is accustomed to direct herself to God, upon every occasion, that, as a flower at sun-rising, conceives a sense of God, in every beam of his, and spreads and dilates itself towards him, in a thankfulness, in every small blessing that he sheds upon her; that soul, that as a flower at the sun's declining, contracts and gathers in, and shuts up herself, as though she had received a blow, whensoever she hears her Saviour wounded by an oath, or blasphemy, or execration; that soul, who, whatsoever string be strucken in her, base or treble, her high or her low estate, is ever tuned toward God, that soul prays sometimes when it does not know that it prays. I hear that man name God, and ask him what said you, and perchance he cannot tell; but I remember that he casts forth some of those *ejaculationes animæ*, (as St Augustine calls them) some of those darts of a devout soul; which, though they have not particular deliberations, and be not formal prayers, yet they are the *indicia*, pregnant evidences and blessed fruits of a religious custom; much more is it true, which St Bernard says there, of them, *Deus audit*, God hears that voice of the heart, which the heart itself hears not, that is, at first considers not. Those occasional and transitory prayers, and those fixed and stationary prayers, for which, many times, we bind ourselves to private prayer at such a time, are payments of this debt, in such pieces, and in such sums, as God, no doubt, accepts at our hands. But yet the solemn days of payment, are the sabbaths of the Lord, and the place of this payment, is the house of the Lord, where, as Tertullian expresses it, *Agmine facto* [forming a line of battle], we muster our forces together, and besiege God; that is, not taking up every tattered fellow, every sudden rag or fragment of speech, that rises from our tongue, or our affections, but mustering up those words, which the Church hath levied for that service, in the confessions, and absolutions, and collects, and litanies of the Church, we pay this debt, and we receive our acquittance.

JOHN DONNE (1572–1631)   47

JORDAN (1)

Who says that fictions only and false hair
Become a verse? Is there in truth no beauty?
Is all good structure in a winding stair?
May no lines pass, except they do their duty
    Not to a true, but painted chair?

Is it no verse, except enchanted groves
And sudden arbours shadow coarse-spun lines?
Must purling streams refresh a lover's loves?
Must all be veil'd, while he that reads, divines,
    Catching the sense at two removes?

Shepherds are honest people; let them sing:
Riddle who list, for me, and pull for Prime:
I envy no man's nightingale or spring;
Nor let them punish me with loss of rhyme,
    Who plainly say, *My God, My King.*

JORDAN (2)

When first my lines of heav'nly joys made mention,
Such was their lustre, they did so excel,
That I sought out quaint words, and trim invention:
My thoughts began to burnish, sprout, and swell,
Curling with metaphors a plain intention,
Decking the sense, as if it were to sell.

Thousands of notions in my brain did run,
Off'ring their service, if I were not sped:
I often blotted what I had begun;
This was not quick enough, and that was dead.
Nothing could seem too rich to clothe the sun,
Much less those joys which trample on his head.

As flames do work and wind, when they ascend,
So did I weave my self into the sense.
But while I bustled, I might hear a friend
Whisper, *How wide is all this long pretence!*
There is in love a sweetness ready penn'd:
Copy out only that, and save expense.

GEORGE HERBERT (1593-1633)

THE DIVINE IMAGE

To Mercy Pity Peace and Love
All pray in their distress,
And to these virtues of delight
Return their thankfulness.

For Mercy Pity Peace and Love
Is God our father dear,
And Mercy Pity Peace and Love
Is Man his child and care.

For Mercy has a human heart,
Pity, a human face,
And Love, the human form divine,
And Peace, the human dress.

Then every man of every clime
That prays in his distress,
Prays to the human form divine,
Love Mercy Pity Peace.

And all must love the human form
In heathen, turk or jew.
Where Mercy Love & Pity dwell
There God is dwelling too.

From THE FOURTH CENTURY

Since Lov will thrust in it self as the Greatest of all
Principles, let us at last willingly allow it Room. I was
once a Stranger to it, now I am familiar with it as a
Daily acquaintance. Tis the only Heir and Benefactor
of the World. It seems it will break in evry where, as
that without which the World could not be Enjoyed.
Nay as that without which it would not be Worthy to
be Enjoyed · for it was Beautified by Lov, and com-
mandeth the Lov of a Donor to us. Lov is a Phœnix that
will revive in its own Ashes, inherit Death, and smell
sweetly in the Grave.

These two properties are in it · that it can attempt all,
and suffer all. And the more it suffers the more it is
Delighted, and the more it attempteth the more it is
enriched · for it seems that all Lov is so Mysterious,
that there is som thing in it which needs Expression,
and can never be understood by any Manifestation,
(of it self, in it self:) but only by Mighty Doings and
Sufferings. This moved GOD the Father to Creat the
World and GOD, the Son to die for it. Nor is this all.
There are many other ways wherby it manifests it self
as well as these · there being still somthing infinit in it
behind. In its Laws in its Tenderness, in its Provisions,
in its Caresses, in its Joys as well as in its Hazzards, in

its Honors as well as in its Cares, nor does it ever ceas till it has poured out it self in all its Communications. In all which it ever rights and satisfies it self. For abov all Things in all Worlds it desires to be Magnified, and taketh pleasure in being Glorified before its Object · for which caus also it does all those Things, which magnify its Object and increase its Happiness.

Whether Lov principaly intends its own Glory, or its Objects Happiness is a Great Question: and of the more importance, becaus the right ordering of our own Affections depends much upon the Solution of it · for on the one side, to be Self Ended is Mercenary, and Base and Slavish, and to do all things for ones own Glory, is servile, and vain Glory. On the other GOD doth all things for Himself, and seeketh his Glory as his last End, and is himself the End whom he seeks and attains in all His Ways. How shall we reconcile this Riddle? or untie this Knot? for som Men hav taken occasion herby seeing this in Lov, to affirm that there is no true Lov in the World. But it is all self Lov whatsoever a Man doth. Implying also that it was self lov in our Savior, that made Him to undertake for us. Wherupon we might justly Question, whether it were more for his own Ends, or more for ours? As also whether it were for his own End that God created the World or more for ours? for Extraordinary much of our Duty and felicity hangeth upon this Point: and whatsoever sword untieth this Gordian Knot, will open a World of Benefit and Instruction to us.

ON PRAYER

In 1938 I spent ten days at Solesmes, from Palm Sunday to Easter Tuesday, following all the liturgical services. I was suffering from splitting headaches; each sound hurt me like a blow; by an extreme effort of concentration I was able to rise above this wretched flesh, to leave it to suffer by itself, heaped up in a corner, and to find a pure and perfect joy in the unimaginable beauty of the chanting and the words. This experience enabled me by analogy to get a better understanding of the possibility of loving divine love in the midst of affliction. It goes without saying that in the course of these services the thought of the Passion of Christ entered into my being once and for all.

There was a young English Catholic there from whom I gained my first idea of the supernatural power of the Sacraments because of the truly angelic radiance with which he seemed to be clothed after going to communion. Chance – for I always prefer saying chance rather than Providence – made of him a messenger to me. For he told me of the existence of those English poets of the seventeenth century who are named metaphysical. In reading them later on, I discovered the poem of which I read you what is unfortunately a very inadequate translation. It is called *Love*. I learnt it by heart. Often, at the culminating point of a violent head-

ache, I make myself say it over, concentrating all my
attention upon it and clinging with all my soul to the
tenderness it enshrines. I used to think I was merely
reciting it as a beautiful poem, but without my knowing it the recitation had the virtue of a prayer. It was
during one of these recitations that, as I told you,
Christ himself came down and took possession of me.

SIMONE WEIL (1909–1943),   55
TRANS. EMMA CRAUFORD

LOVE

Love bade me welcome; yet my soul drew back,
    Guilty of dust and sin.
But quick-eyed Love, observing me grow slack
    From my first entrance in,
Drew nearer to me, sweetly questioning
    If I lack'd anything.

'A guest,' I answer'd, 'worthy to be here:'
    Love said, 'You shall be he.'
'I, the unkind, ungrateful? Ah, my dear,
    I cannot look on Thee.'
Love took my hand and smiling did reply,
    'Who made the eyes but I?'

'Truth, Lord, but I have marr'd them: let my shame
    Go where it doth deserve.'
'And know you not,' says Love, 'Who bore the blame?'
    'My dear, then I will serve.'
'You must sit down,' says Love, 'and taste my meat.'
    So I did sit and eat.

PRIME

AWAKE, MY SOUL

Awake, my soul, and with the sun
Thy daily stage of duty run;
Shake off dull sloth, and joyful rise
To pay thy morning sacrifice.

Redeem thy mis-spent moments past,
And live this day as if thy last;
Improve thy talent with due care;
For the great day thyself prepare.

Let all thy converse be sincere,
Thy conscience as the noonday clear;
Think how all-seeing God thy ways
And all thy secret thoughts surveys.

Lord, I my vows to thee renew;
Scatter my sins as morning dew;
Guard my first springs of thought and will,
And with thyself my spirit fill.

Direct, control, suggest, this day,
All I design, or do, or say;
That all my powers, with all their might,
In thy sole glory may unite.

Praise God from whom all blessings flow;
Praise him, all creatures here below;
Praise him above, ye heavenly host;
Praise Father, Son, and Holy Ghost.

From KILVERT'S DIARY

Monday, 11 July, 1870
The view from my bedroom window looking up the dingle always reminds me of Norway, perhaps because of the spiry dark fir tops which rise above the lighter green trees. Often when I rise I look up to the white farm house of Penllan and think of the sweet grey eyes that have long been open and looking upon the pearly morning sky and the mists of the valley and the morning spread upon the mountains, and think of the young busy hands that have long been at work, milking or churning, with the sleeves rolled up the round arms as white and creamy as the milk itself, and the bright sweet morning face that the sunrise and the fresh early air have kissed into bloom and the sunny tresses ruffled by the mountain wind, and hope that the fatherless girl may ever be good, brave, pure and true. So help her God. The sun looks through her window which the great pear tree frames and lattices in green leaves and fruit, and the leaves move and flicker and throw a chequering shadow upon the white bedroom wall, and on the white curtains of the bed. And before the sun has touched the sleeping village in the shade below or has even struck the weathercock into a golden gleam, or has crept down the steep green slope of the lower or upper Bron, he has stolen into her bedroom and crept along

the wall from chair to chair till he has reached the bed, and has kissed the fair hand and arm that lies upon the coverlet and the white bosom that heaves half uncovered after the restlessness of the sultry night, and has kissed her mouth whose scarlet lips, just parting in a smile and pouting like rosebuds to be kissed, show the pearly gleam of the white teeth, and has kissed the sweet face and the blue veined silky lashed eyelids and the white brow and the soft bright tangled hair, till she has unclosed the sweetest eyes that ever opened to the dawn, and risen and unfastened the casement and stood awhile breathing the fresh fragrant mountain air as it blows cool upon her flushed cheek and her half veiled bosom, and lifts and ruffles her bright hair which still keeps the kiss of the sun. Then when she has dressed and prayed towards the east, she goes out to draw water from the holy spring St Mary's Well. After which she goes about her honest holy work, all day long, with a light heart and a pure conscience.

PIED BEAUTY

Glory be to God for dappled things –
    For skies of couple-colour as a brinded cow;
      For rose-moles all in stipple upon trout that
          swim;
Fresh-firecoal chestnut-falls; finches' wings;
    Landscape plotted and pieced – fold, fallow, and
          plough;
      And áll trádes, their gear and tackle and trim.

All things counter, original, spare, strange;
    Whatever is fickle, freckled (who knows how?)
      With swift, slow; sweet, sour; adazzle, dim;
He fathers-forth whose beauty is past change:
                    Praise him.

O GOD, EARLY IN THE MORNING
I CRY TO YOU

O God, early in the morning I cry to you.
Help me to pray
And to concentrate my thoughts on you:
I cannot do this alone.

In me there is darkness,
But with you there is light;
I am lonely, but you do not leave me;
I am feeble in heart, but with you there is help;
I am restless, but with you there is peace.
In me there is bitterness, but with you there is
        patience;
I do not understand your ways,
But you know the way for me . . .

Restore me to liberty,
And enable me so to live now
That I may answer before you and before me.
Lord, whatever this day may bring,
Your name be praised.

MORNING HYMN

New every morning is the love
Our wakening and uprising prove;
Through sleep and darkness safely brought,
Restored to life, and power, and thought.

New mercies, each returning day,
Hover around us while we pray;
New perils past, new sins forgiven,
New thoughts of God, new hopes of heaven.

If, on our daily course, our mind
Be set to hallow all we find,
New treasures still, of countless price,
God will provide for sacrifice.

The trivial round, the common task,
Will furnish all we ought to ask;
Room to deny ourselves, a road
To bring us daily nearer God.

Only, O Lord, in thy dear love
Fit us for perfect rest above;
And help us this and every day
To live more nearly as we pray.

JOHN KEBLE (1792–1866)

GOD STRENGTHEN ME

God strengthen me to bear myself;
That heaviest weight of all to bear,
Inalienable weight of care ...

If I could once lay down myself,
And start self-purged upon the race
That all must run! Death runs apace.

If I could set aside myself,
And start with lightened heart upon
The road by all men overgone!

God harden me against myself,
This coward with pathetic voice
Who craves for ease, and rest and joys:

Myself, arch-traitor to myself,
My hollowest friend, my deadliest foe
My clog whatever road I go.

Yet One there is can curb myself,
Can roll the strangling load from me,
Break off the yoke and set me free.

A PRAYER AT MORNING

Cold, slow, silent, but returning, after so many hours.
The sight of something outside me, the day is
      breaking.
May salt, this one day, be sharp upon my tongue;
May I sleep, this one night, without waking.

FORTH IN THY NAME, O LORD, I GO

Forth in thy name, O Lord, I go,
  My daily labour to pursue,
Thee, only thee, resolved to know,
  In all I think, or speak, or do.

The task thy wisdom hath assigned
  O let me cheerfully fulfil;
In all my works thy presence find,
  And prove thy good and perfect will.

Thee may I set at my right hand,
  Whose eyes my inmost substance see,
And labour on at thy command,
  And offer all my works to thee.

Give me to bear thy easy yoke,
  And every moment watch and pray,
And still to things eternal look,
  And hasten to thy glorious day;

For thee delightfully employ
  Whate'er thy bounteous grace hath given;
And run my course with even joy,
  And closely walk with thee to heaven.

PRIME

Simultaneously, as soundlessly,
  Spontaneously, suddenly
As, at the vaunt of the dawn, the kind
  Gates of the body fly open
To its world beyond, the gates of the mind,
  The horn gate and the ivory gate
Swing to, swing shut, instantaneously
  Quell the nocturnal rummage
Of its rebellious fronde, ill-favored,
  Ill-natured and second-rate,
Disenfranchised, widowed and orphaned
  By an historical mistake:
Recalled from the shades to be a seeing being,
  From absence to be on display,
Without a name or history I wake
  Between my body and the day.

Holy this moment, wholly in the right,
  As, in complete obedience
To the light's laconic outcry, next
  As a sheet, near as a wall,
Out there as a mountain's poise of stone,
  The world is present, about,
And I know that I am, here, not alone
  But with a world and rejoice

Unvexed, for the will has still to claim
    This adjacent arm as my own,
The memory to name me, resume
    Its routine of praise and blame,
And smiling to me is this instant while
    Still the day is intact, and I
The Adam sinless in our beginning,
    Adam still previous to any act.

I draw breath; that is of course to wish
    No matter what, to be wise,
To be different, to die and the cost,
    No matter how, is Paradise
Lost of course and myself owing a death:
    The eager ridge, the steady sea,
The flat roofs of the fishing village
    Still asleep in its bunny,
Though as fresh and sunny still, are not friends
    But things to hand, this ready flesh
No honest equal, but my accomplice now,
    My assassin to be, and my name
Stands for my historical share of care
    For a lying self-made city,
Afraid of our living task, the dying
    Which the coming day will ask.

LORD OF FIRE AND DEATH
From THE BHAGAVAD-GĪTĀ

Lord of fire and death, of wind and moon and waters,
Father of the born, and this world's father's Father.
Hail, all hail to you – a thousand salutations.

Take our salutations, Lord, from every quarter,
Infinite of might and boundless in your glory,
You are all that is, since everywhere we find you ...

Author of this world, the unmoved and the moving,
You alone are fit for worship, you the highest.
Where in the three worlds shall any find your equal?

Therefore I bow down, prostrate and ask for pardon:
Now forgive me, God, as friend forgives his comrade,
Father forgives son, and man his dearest lover.

ANON. (5TH–2ND CENTURY BC),
TRANS. SWAMI PRABHAVANANDA

JEWISH PRAYER

Though our mouths were full of song as the sea,
Our tongues of exultation as the fullness of its waves,
And our lips of praise as the plains of the firmament:

Though our eyes gave light as the sun and moon:
Though our hands were outspread as the eagles of
  heaven,
And our feet were swift as hinds,

Yet should we be unable to thank Thee,
O Lord our God and God of our fathers,
And to bless Thy Name for even one of the countless
  thousands
And tens of thousands
Of kindnesses which Thou hast done by our fathers
  and by us.

GREAT AND HOLY IS THE LORD
From THE DEAD SEA SCROLLS

Great and holy is the Lord,
 the holiest of holy ones for every generation.
Majesty precedes him,
 and following him is the rush of many waters.
Grace and truth surround his presence;
 truth and justice and righteousness are the
   foundation of his throne.
Separating light from deep darkness,
 by the knowledge of his mind he established the
   dawn.
When all his angels had witnessed it they sang aloud;
 for he showed them what they had not known;
Crowning the hills with fruit,
 good food for every living being.
Blessed be he who makes the earth by his power
 establishing the world in his wisdom.
In his understanding he stretched out the heavens,
 and brought forth wind from his storehouses.
He made lightning for the rain,
 and caused mists to rise from the end of the earth.

ANON. (*c.* 1ST CENTURY AD)   73

GASCOIGNE'S GOOD-MORROW

You that have spent the silent night
In sleep and quiet rest,
And joy to see the cheerful light
That riseth in the east,
Now clear your voice, now cheer your heart,
Come help me now to sing;
Each willing wight come bear a part
To praise the heavenly King.

And you whom care in prison keeps,
Or sickness doth suppress,
Or secret sorrow breaks your sleeps,
Or dolours do distress –
Yet bear a part in doleful wise,
Yea think it good accord
And acceptable sacrifice,
Each sprite to praise the Lord.

The dreadful night with darksomeness
Had overspread the light,
And sluggish sleep with drowsiness
Had overpressed our might:
A glass wherein you may behold
Each storm that stops our breath –
Our bed the grave, our clothes like mould,
And sleep like dreadful death.

Yet as this deadly night did last
But for a little space,
And heavenly day now night is past
Doth show his pleasant face,
So must we hope to see God's face
At last in Heaven on high,
When we have changed this mortal place
For immortality.

And of such haps and heavenly joys
As then we hope to hold,
All earthly sights and worldly toys
Are tokens to behold:
The day is like the day of doom;
The sun, the Son of man;
The skies, the heavens; the earth, the tomb
Wherein we rest till then;

The rainbow bending in the sky,
Bedecked with sundry hues,
Is like the seat of God on high,
And seems to tell these news –
That as thereby he promisèd
To drown the world no more,
So by the blood which Christ hath shed
He will our health restore.

The misty clouds that fall sometime
And overcast the skies
Are like to troubles of our time
Which do but dim our eyes;
But as such dews are dried up quite
When Phoebus shows his face,
So are such fancies put to flight
Where God doth guide by grace.

The carrion crow, that loathsome beast
Which cries against the rain,
Both for her hue and for the rest
The Devil resembleth plain;
And as with guns we kill the crow
For spoiling our relief,
The Devil so must we overthrow
With gunshot of belief.

The little birds which sing so sweet
Are like the angels' voice
Which render God his praises meet,
And teach us to rejoice;
And as they more esteem that mirth
Than dread the night's annoy,
So must we deem our days on earth
But hell to heavenly joy –

Unto which joys for to attain
God grant us all his grace,
And send us after worldly pain
In Heaven to have a place,
Where we may still enjoy that light
Which never shall decay.
Lord, for thy mercy lend us might
To see that joyful day.

GEORGE GASCOIGNE (1542–1577)   77

THE DIVINE LOVER

*'Wherefore hidest Thou Thy face and holdest me for
Thine enemy?'*

Why dost Thou shade Thy lovely face? O why
Does that eclipsing hand so long deny
The sunshine of Thy soul-enliv'ning eye?

Without that Light, what light remains in me?
Thou art my Life, my Way, my Light; in Thee
I live, I move, and by Thy beams I see.

Thou art my Life; if Thou but turn away,
My life's a thousand deaths: Thou art my Way;
Without Thee, Lord, I travel not, but stray.

My Light Thou art; without Thy glorious sight,
Mine eyes are darkened with perpetual night.
My God, Thou art my Way, my Life, my Light.

Thou art my Way; I wander, if Thou fly:
Thou art my Light; if hid, how blind am I!
Thou art my Life; If Thou withdraw, I die.

Mine eyes are blind and dark, I cannot see;
To whom, or whither, should my darkness flee,
But to the Light? And who's that Light but Thee?

My path is lost; my wandering steps do stray;
I cannot safely go, nor safely stay;
Whom should I seek but Thee, my Path, my Way?

.   .   .

If I have lost my Path, great Shepherd say,
Shall I still wander in a doubtful way?
Lord, shall a lamb of Israel's sheepfold stray?

Thou art the pilgrim's Path; the blind man's Eye;
The dead man's Life; on Thee my hopes rely;
If Thou remove, I err, I grope, I die.

Disclose Thy sun-beams; close Thy wings, and stay;
See, see how I am blind, and dead, and stray,
O Thou, that art my Light, my Life, my Way.

O LORD, IN MERCY GRANT MY SOUL
TO LIVE

O Lord, in Mercy grant my soul to live,
And patience grant, that hurt I may not grieve:
    How shall I know what thing is best to seek?
Thou only knowest: what Thou knowest, give!

AL-ANSARI (*d.* 1088)

From THE KORAN

In God's Name be the course and the mooring: let us
    embark.

SURAH 11. 41: PRAYER OF NOAH (*c.* 6TH CENTURY AD),
TRANS. M. PICKTHALL

TIERCE

THE PILGRIM SONG

Who would true Valour see,
Let him come hither;
One here will Constant be,
Come Wind, come Weather.
There's no Discouragement
Shall make him once Relent
His first avow'd Intent
To be a Pilgrim.

Whoso beset him round
With dismal Stories,
Do but themselves Confound;
His strength the more is.
No Lyon can him fright,
He'll with a Giant fight,
But he will have a right
To be a Pilgrim.

Hobgoblin, nor foul Fiend,
Can daunt his Spirit:
He knows, he at the end
Shall Life Inherit.
Then Fancies fly away,
He'll fear not what men say,
He'll labour Night and Day
To be a Pilgrim.

JOHN BUNYAN (1626–1688)

ON HIS BLINDNESS

When I consider how my light is spent
   Ere half my days in this dark world and wide,
   And that one talent which is death to hide
   Lodged with me useless, though my soul more bent
To serve therewith my maker, and present
   My true account, lest he returning chide,
   'Doth God exact day-labour, light denied?'
I fondly ask. But Patience, to prevent
That murmur, soon replies, 'God doth not need
   Either man's work or his own gifts; who best
   Bear his mild yoke, they serve him best: his state
Is kingly. Thousands at his bidding speed,
   And post o'er land and ocean without rest;
   They also serve who only stand and wait.'

JOHN MILTON (1608–1674)

ARABIC PRAYER

It is glory enough for me
That I should be Your servant
It is grace enough for me
That You should be my Lord.

84   ANON.

THE DEED

Lord, not for light in darkness do we pray,
Not that the veil be lifted from our eyes,
Nor that the slow ascension of our day
        Be otherwise.

Not for a clearer vision of the things
Whereof the fashioning shall make us great,
Not for remission of the peril and stings
        Of time and fate.

Not for a fuller knowledge of the end
Whereto we travel, bruised yet unafraid,
Nor that the little healing that we lend
        Shall be repaid.

Not these, O Lord. We would not break the bars
Thy wisdom sets about us; we shall climb
Unfetter'd to the secrets of the stars
        In Thy good time.

We do not crave the high perception swift
When to refrain were well, and when fulfil,
Nor yet the understanding strong to sift
        The good from ill.

Not these, O Lord. For these Thou hast reveal'd,
We know the golden season when to reap
The heavy-fruited treasure of the field,
    The hour to sleep.

Not these. We know the hemlock from the rose,
The pure from stain'd, the noble from the base,
The tranquil holy light of truth that glows
    On Pity's face.

We know the paths wherein our feet should press,
Across our hearts are written Thy decrees:
Yet now, O Lord, be merciful to bless
    With more than these.

Grant us the will to fashion as we feel,
Grant us the strength to labour as we know,
Grant us the purpose, ribb'd and edged with steel,
    To strike the blow.

Knowledge we ask not – knowledge Thou hast lent,
But, Lord, the will – there lies our bitter need,
Give us to build above the deep intent
    The deed, the deed.

OBEDIENCE

Dearest Lord, teach me to be generous;
Teach me to serve thee as thou deservest;
To give and not to count the cost,
To fight and not to heed the wounds,
To toil and not to seek for rest,
To labour and not to seek reward,
Save that of knowing that I do thy will.

ST IGNATIUS LOYOLA (1491–1556)

PRAYER

Make us worthy, Lord,
To serve our fellow-men
Throughout the world who live and die
In poverty or hunger.

Give them, through our hands
This day their daily bread,
And by our understanding love,
Give peace and joy.

MOTHER TERESA, CALCUTTA (1910–   )

FOR THE POOR

But beggars about midsummer go breadless to supper,
And winter is yet worse, for they are wet-shod
    wanderers,
Frozen and famished and foully challenged
And berated by rich men so that it is rueful to listen.
Now Lord, send them summer or some manner of
    happiness
After their going hence for what they have here
    suffered.
For thou mightest have made us equal, none meaner
    than another,
With equal wit and wisdom, if such had been thy
    wishes.
Have ruth on these rich men who reward not thy
    prisoners;
Many are *ingrati* of the good that thou hast given
    them.
But God, in thy goodness, grant them grace of
    amendment.
For they dread no dearth nor drought nor freshets,
Nor heat nor hail, if they have their comfort.
Nothing is wanting to them here of what they wish and
    will.
But poor people, thy prisoners, Lord, in the pit of
    misery,

Comfort thy creatures who have such a care to suffer
Through dearth, through drought, all their days here.
Woe in winter for want of clothing!
Who seldom in summer-time sup fully!
Comfort thy careworn, Christ, in thy riches.

WILLIAM LANGLAND (*c.* 1330–1386),
TRANS. NEVILLE COGHILL

LORD, MAKE ME AN INSTRUMENT OF THY PEACE

Lord, make me an instrument of Thy peace.
Where there is hatred, let me sow love;
Where there is injury, pardon;
Where there is doubt, faith;
When there is despair, hope;
Where there is darkness, light;
When there is sadness, joy.

O Divine Master, grant that
I may not so much seek
To be consoled, as to console;
Not so much to be understood as
To understand; not so much to be
Loved as to love:
For it is in giving that we receive;
It is in pardoning, that we are pardoned;
It is in dying, that we awaken to eternal life.

ON TRUST IN THE HEART

The Perfect Way is only difficult for those who pick
    and choose.
Do not like, do not dislike: all will then be clear.
Make a hairbreadth of difference, and Heaven and
    Earth are set apart.
If you want truth to stand clear before you, never be
    for or against.
The struggle between 'like' and 'dislike' is the mind's
    worst disease.
While the deep meaning is misunderstood, it is useless
    to meditate on tranquillity.
The Buddha-nature is featureless as space: it has no
    'too little' or 'too much'.
Only because we take and reject does it seem to us not
    to be so . . .

SENGTS'AN (*c.* AD 606),
TRANS. ARTHUR WALEY

CHARITY'S CHILD

As proud of a penny as of a pound of gold,
And as glad of a garment of russet grey
As of a silken tunic of scarlet tint.
He rejoices with the joyful, and is generous to the
    wicked,
Loving and believing in all that our Lord made ...
All manner of mischiefs he mildly suffers,
Coveting no earthly good, but the joy of heaven.
Fiat voluntas tua will always find him.
He tends, at other times, to take a pilgrimage
To seek pardon of the poor, and of those in prison.
Though he brings them no bread, he bears them
    sweeter life,
Loving them as our Lord has bidden, looking how they
    are ...
For Charity is God's champion, a cheerful child,
The merriest of mouth when he sits at meat.
The love that lies in his heart has made him light of
    speech,
Comforting and companionable, as Christ Himself bade.
I have seen him in silk, and in coarsest cloth,
Grey or gaudy, or in gilt harness,
And as gladly he gave it to good fellows needing it ...
And in a friar's frock he was found once,
But it was far away, in Saint Francis' time ...

92   WILLIAM LANGLAND (*c.* 1330–1386),
       TRANS. NEVILLE COGHILL

DOXOLOGY

Great God accept our gratitude,
    For the great gifts on us bestowed –
For Raiment, shelter and for food.

Great God, our gratitude we bring,
    Accept our humble offering,
For all the gifts on us bestowed,
    Thy name be evermore adored.

JOSEPHINE DELPHINE
HENDERSON HEARD (1861–1921)

THE LATEST DECALOGUE

Thou shalt have one God only; who
Would be at the expense of two?
No graven images may be
Worshipped, except the currency:
Swear not at all; for, for thy curse
Thine enemy is none the worse:
At church on Sunday to attend
Will serve to keep the world thy friend:
Honour thy parents; that is, all
From whom advancement may befall;
Thou shalt not kill; but need'st not strive
Officiously to keep alive:
Do not adultery commit;
Advantage rarely comes of it:
Thou shalt not steal; an empty feat,
When it's so lucrative to cheat:
Bear not false witness; let the lie
Have time on its own wings to fly:
Thou shalt not covet, but tradition
Approves all forms of competition.

HIS CREED

I do believe, that die I must,
And be return'd from out my dust:
I do believe, that when I rise,
Christ I shall see, with these same eyes:
I do believe, that I must come,
With others, to the dreadfull Doome:
I do believe, the bad must goe
From thence, to everlasting woe:

I do believe, the good, and I,
Shall live with Him eternally:
I do believe, I shall inherit
Heaven, by Christs mercies, not my merit:
I do believe, the One in Three,
And Three in perfect Unitie:
Lastly, that JESUS is a Deed
Of Gift from God: *And heres my Creed.*

ROBERT HERRICK (1591–1674)   95

HYMN TO MATTER

Blessed be you, harsh matter, barren soil, stubborn rock: you who yield only to violence, you who force us to work if we would eat. Blessed be you, perilous matter, violent sea, untameable passion: you who unless we fetter you will devour us. Blessed be you, mighty matter, irresistible march of evolution, reality ever new-born; you who, by constantly shattering our mental categories, force us to go ever further and further in our pursuit of the truth. Blessed be you, universal matter, unmeasurable time, boundless ether, triple abyss of stars and atoms and generations: you who by overflowing and dissolving our narrow standards of measurement reveal to us the dimensions of God ...

TEILHARD DE CHARDIN (1881–1955),
TRANS. BERNARD WALL

GOD'S GRANDEUR

The world is charged with the grandeur of God.
   It will flame out, like shining from shook foil;
   It gathers to a greatness, like the ooze of oil
Crushed. Why do men then now not reck his rod?
Generations have trod, have trod, have trod;
   And all is seared with trade; bleared, smeared with
         toil;
   And wears man's smudge and shares man's smell:
         the soil
Is bare now, nor can foot feel, being shod.

And for all this, nature is never spent;
   There lives the dearest freshness deep down things;
And though the last lights off the black West went
   Oh, morning, at the brown brink eastward, springs –
Because the Holy Ghost over the bent
   World broods with warm breast and with ah! bright
         wings.

THY KINGDOM COME

Thy kingdom come. That is, may your reign be realised here, as it is realised there. But I tend to take *there* on three levels. First, as in the sinless world beyond the horrors of animal and human life; in the behaviour of stars and trees and water, in sunrise and wind. May there be *here* (in my heart) the beginning of a like beauty. Secondly, as in the best human lives I have known: in all the people who really bear the burdens and ring true, the people we call bricks, and in the quiet, busy, ordered life of really good families and really good religious houses. May that too be 'here'. Finally, of course, in the usual sense: as in heaven, as among the blessed dead.

And *here* can of course be taken not only for 'in my heart', but for 'in this college' – in England – in the world in general. But prayer is not the time for pressing our own favourite social or political panacea. Even Queen Victoria didn't like 'being talked to as if she were a public meeting'.

Thy will be done. My festoons on this have been added gradually. At first I took it exclusively as an act of submission, attempting to do with it what Our Lord did in Gethsemane. I thought of God's will purely as something that would come upon me, something of which I should be the patient. And I also thought of it as a will which would be embodied in pains and disappointments. Not, to be sure, that I suppose God's will for me to consist entirely of disagreeables. But I thought it was only the disagreeables that called for this preliminary submission – the agreeables could look after themselves for the present. When they turned up, one could give thanks.

This interpretation is, I expect, the commonest. And so it must be. And such are the miseries of human life that it must often fill our whole mind. But at other times other meanings can be added. So I added one more.

The peg for it is, I admit, much more obvious in the English version than in the Greek or Latin. No matter: this is where the liberty of festooning comes in. 'Thy will *be done*'. But a great deal of it is to be done by God's creatures; including me. The petition, then, is not merely that I may patiently suffer God's will but also that I may vigorously do it. I must be an agent as well as a patient. I am asking that I may be enabled to do it. In the long run I am asking to be given 'the same mind which was also in Christ'.

Taken this way, I find the words have a more regular daily application. For there isn't always – or we don't always have reason to suspect that there is – some great affliction looming in the near future, but there are always duties to be done; usually, for me, neglected duties to be caught up with. 'Thy will be *done* – by me – now' brings one back to brass tacks.

C. S. LEWIS (1898–1963)   99

LET ME SEEK YOU BY DESIRING YOU

Lord Jesus Christ; Let me seek you by desiring you,
　　and let me desire you by seeking you;
　　let me find you by loving you,
　　and love you in finding you.

　　I confess, Lord, with thanksgiving,
　　that you have made me in your image,
so that I can remember you, think of you, and love you.
But that image is so worn and blotted out by faults,
　　and darkened by the smoke of sin,
　　that it cannot do that for which it was made,
　　unless you renew and refashion it.
Lord, I am not trying to make my way to your height,
for my understanding is in no way equal to that,
but I do desire to understand a little of your truth
　　which my heart already believes and loves.
I do not seek to understand so that I can believe,
　　but I believe so that I may understand;
　　　　and what is more,
I believe that unless I do believe, I shall not
　　　　understand.

　　ST ANSELM (1033?–1109),
　　　TRANS. BENEDICTA WARD

CANTICA
Our Lord Christ: of order

Set Love in order, thou that lovest Me.
   Never was virtue out of order found;
And though I fill thy heart desirously,
   By thine own virtue I must keep My ground:
When to My love thou dost bring charity,
   Even she must come with order girt and gown'd.
      Look how the trees are bound
      To order, bearing fruit;
      And by one thing compute,
In all things earthly, order's grace or gain.

All earthly things I had the making of
   Were number'd and were measured then by Me;
And each was order'd to its end by Love,
   Each kept, through order, clean for ministry.
Charity most of all, when known enough,
   Is of her very nature orderly.
      Lo, now! what heat in thee,
      Soul, can have bred this rout?
      Thou putt'st all order out.
Even this love's heat must be its curb and rein.

ST FRANCIS OF ASSISI (1181/2–1226),   101
TRANS. D. G. ROSSETTI

O THOU WHO CAMEST FROM ABOVE

O thou who camest from above,
The pure celestial fire to impart,
Kindle a flame of sacred love
On the mean altar of my heart.

There let it for thy glory burn
With inextinguishable blaze,
And trembling to its source return
In humble prayer, and fervent praise.

Jesus, confirm my heart's desire
To work, and speak, and think for thee;
Still let me guard the holy fire,
And still stir up thy gift in me.

Ready for all thy perfect will,
My acts of faith and love repeat,
Till death thy endless mercies seal,
And make my sacrifice complete.

GRANT TO ME, O LORD

Grant to me, O Lord, to know what I ought to know, to love what I ought to love, to praise what delights Thee most, to value what is precious in thy sight, to hate what is offensive to Thee. Do not suffer me to judge according to the sight of my eyes, nor to pass sentence according to the hearing of the ears of ignorant men; but to discern with true judgement between things visible and spiritual, and above all things to enquire what is the good pleasure of thy will.

THOMAS À KEMPIS (1380–1471)

CLOSE MINE EYES FROM EVIL

Close mine eyes from evil,
And my ears from hearing idle words,
And my heart from reflecting on unchaste thoughts,
And my veins from thinking of transgression.

Guide my feet to walk in thy commandments
And thy righteous ways,
And may thy mercies be turned upon me.

BERAKOTH (DATE UNKNOWN)

ACTIVE PASSIVITY

It is at those moments when we are, as we say, in a bad mood, when we feel incapable of the elevation of soul which befits holy things, it is then that it is most effectual to turn our eyes towards perfect purity. For it is then that evil, or rather mediocrity, comes to the surface of the soul and is in the best position for being burnt by contact with the fire.

It is however then that the act of looking is almost impossible. All the mediocre part of the soul, fearing death with a more violent fear than that caused by the approach of the death of the body, revolts and suggests lies to protect itself.

The effort not to listen to these lies, although we cannot prevent ourselves from believing them, the effort to look upon purity at such times, has to be something very violent; yet it is absolutely different from all that is generally known as effort, such as doing violence to one's feelings or an act of will. Other words are needed to express it, but language cannot provide them.

The effort which brings a soul to salvation is like the effort of looking or of listening; it is the kind of effort by which a fiancée accepts her lover. It is an act of attention and consent; whereas what language designates as will is something suggestive of muscular effort.

The will is on the level of the natural part of the soul. The right use of the will is a condition of salvation, necessary no doubt but remote, inferior, very subordinate and purely negative. The weeds are pulled up by the muscular effort of the peasant, but only sun and water can make the corn grow. The will cannot produce any good in the soul.

Efforts of the will are only in their right place for carrying out definite obligations. Wherever there is no strict obligation we must follow either our natural inclination or our vocation, that is to say God's command. Actions prompted by our inclination clearly do not involve an effort of will. In our acts of obedience to God we are passive; whatever difficulties we have to surmount, however great our activity may appear to be, there is nothing analogous to muscular effort; there is only waiting, attention, silence, immobility, constant through suffering and joy. The crucifixion of Christ is the model of all acts of obedience.

This kind of passive activity, the highest of all, is perfectly described in the *Baghavat-Gita* and in Lao-Tse. Also there is a supernatural union of opposites, a harmony in the Pythagorean sense.

That we have to strive after goodness with an effort of our will is one of the lies invented by the mediocre part of ourselves in its fear of being destroyed. Such an effort does not threaten it in any way, it does not even disturb its comfort – not even when it entails a great deal of fatigue and suffering. For the mediocre part of ourselves is not afraid of fatigue and suffering, it is afraid of being killed.

There are people who try to raise their souls like a man continually taking standing jumps in the hope that, if he jumps higher every day, a time may come when he will no longer fall back but will go right up to the sky. Thus occupied he cannot look at the sky. We cannot take a single step towards heaven. It is not in our power to travel in a vertical direction. If however we look heavenwards for a long time, God comes and takes us up. He raises us easily. As Æschylus says: 'There is no effort in what is divine.' There is an easiness in salvation which is more difficult for us than all our efforts.

SIMONE WEIL (1909–1943),
TRANS. EMMA CRAUFURD

LONG-SUFFERING OF GOD

One hundred feet from off the ground
    That noble Aloe blows;
But mark ye by what skill profound
    His charming grandeur rose.

One hundred years of patient care
    The gardners did bestow,
Toil and hereditary pray'r
    Made all this glorious show.

Thus man goes on from year to year,
    And bears no fruit at all;
But gracious God, still unsevere,
    Bids show'rs of blessings fall.

The beams of mercy, dews of grace,
    Our Saviour still supplies –
Ha! ha! the soul regains her place,
    And sweetens all the skies.

CHRISTOPHER SMART (1722–1771)

LIGHT SHINING OUT OF DARKNESS

God moves in a mysterious way
    His wonders to perform;
He plants His footsteps in the sea,
    And rides upon the storm.

Deep in unfathomable mines
    Of never failing skill
He treasures up His bright designs,
    And works His sovereign will.

Ye fearful saints, fresh courage take:
    The clouds ye so much dread
Are big with mercy, and shall break
    In blessings on your head.

Judge not the Lord by feeble sense,
    But trust Him for His grace;
Behind a frowning providence
    He hides a smiling face.

His purposes will ripen fast,
    Unfolding ev'ry hour;
The bud may have a bitter taste,
    But sweet will be the flow'r.

Blind unbelief is sure to err,
    And scan His work in vain;
God is His own interpreter,
    And He will make it plain.

SIX PRAYERS FROM AN INDIAN PEASANT

THE SENSE OF SIN

Lord, I have abandoned all for Thee,
Yet evermore desire riseth in my heart,
And maketh me forget Thy love:

Ah, save me, save me,
Save me by Thyself:

As thus I bow before Thee, Lord,
Come dwell within,
Live Thou Thy secret life in me,
And save me by Thyself.

MAN'S NEED OF GRACE
As a fish that is dragged from the water
Gaspeth,
So gaspeth my soul:

As one who hath buried his treasure,
And now cannot find the place,
So is my mind distraught:

As a child that hath lost his mother,
So am I troubled, my heart is seared with sore anguish:

O merciful God,
Thou knowest my need,
Come, save me, and show me Thy love.

Of what avail this restless, hurrying activity?
This heavy weight of earthly duties?

God's purposes stand firm,
And thou, His little one,
Needest one thing alone,
Trust in His power, and will, to meet Thy need:

Thy burden resteth safe on Him,
And thou, His little one,
Mayest play securely at His side:

This is the sum and substance of it all –
God is,
God loveth thee,
God beareth all thy care.

GOD'S LIFE WITHIN
Take Lord, unto Thyself,
My sense of self: and let it vanish utterly:

Take, Lord, my life,
Live Thou Thy life through me:

I live no longer, Lord,
But in me now
Thou livest:

Aye, between Thee and me, my God,
There is no longer room for 'I' and 'mine'.

LOVE FOR GOD
Ah, Lord, the torment of this task that Thou hast laid
        on me
To tell the splendour of Thy love!

I sing, and sing,
Yet all the while the truth evadeth telling:

No words there are, no words,
To show Thee as Thou art:

These songs of mine are chaff,
No spark of living truth hath ever lit my lips:

Ah, Lord, the torment of this task that Thou hast laid
     on me!

No deeds I've done nor thoughts I've thought;
Save as Thy servant, I am nought.

Guard me, O God, and O, control
The tumult of my restless soul.

Ah, do not, do not cast on me
The guilt of mine iniquity.

My countless sins, I, Tuka, say,
Upon Thy loving heart I lay.

RESOLUTION AND INDEPENDENCE

There was a roaring in the wind all night;
The rain came heavily and fell in floods;
But now the sun is rising calm and bright;
The birds are singing in the distant woods;
Over his own sweet voice the stock-dove broods;
The jay makes answer as the magpie chatters;
And all the air is filled with pleasant noise of waters.

All things that love the sun are out of doors;
The sky rejoices in the morning's birth;
The grass is bright with rain-drops; – on the moors
The hare is running races in her mirth;
And with her feet she from the plashy earth
Raises a mist that, glittering in the sun,
Runs with her all the way, wherever she doth run.

I was a Traveller then upon the moor;
I saw the hare that raced about with joy;
I heard the woods and distant waters roar;
Or heard them not, as happy as a boy:
The pleasant season did my heart employ:
My old remembrances went from me wholly;
And all the ways of men, so vain and melancholy.

But, as it sometimes chanceth, from the might
Of joy in minds that can no further go,
As high as we have mounted in delight
In our dejection do we sink as low;
To me that morning did it happen so;
And fears and fancies thick upon me came;
Dim sadness – and blind thoughts, I knew not, nor
      could name.

I heard the sky-lark warbling in the sky;
And I bethought me of the playful hare:
Even such a happy Child of earth am I;
Even as these blissful creatures do I fare;
Far from the world I walk, and from all care;
But there may come another day to me –
Solitude, pain of heart, distress, and poverty.

My whole life I have lived in pleasant thought,
As if life's business were a summer mood;
As if all needful things would come unsought
To genial faith, still rich in genial good;
But how can he expect that others should
Build for him, sow for him, and at his call
Love him, who for himself will take no heed at all?

I thought of Chatterton, the marvellous Boy,
The sleepless Soul that perished in his pride;
Of Him who walked in glory and in joy
Following his plough, along the mountain-side:
By our own spirits are we deified:
We Poets in our youth begin in gladness;
But thereof come in the end despondency and madness.

Now, whether it were by peculiar grace,
A leading from above, a something given,
Yet it befell that, in this lonely place,
When I with these untoward thoughts had striven,
Beside a pool bare to the eye of heaven
I saw a Man before me unawares:
The oldest man he seemed that ever wore grey hairs.

As a huge stone is sometimes seen to lie
Couched on the bald top of an eminence;
Wonder to all who do the same espy,
By what means it could thither come, and whence;
So that it seems a thing endued with sense:
Like a sea-beast crawled forth, that on a shelf
Of rock or sand reposeth, there to sun itself;

Such seemed this Man, not all alive nor dead,
Nor all asleep – in his extreme old age:
His body was bent double, feet and head
Coming together in life's pilgrimage;
As if some dire constraint of pain, or rage
Of sickness felt by him in times long past,
A more than human weight upon his frame had cast.

Himself he propped, limbs, body, and pale face,
Upon a long grey staff of shaven wood:
And, still as I drew near with gentle pace,
Upon the margin of that moorish flood
Motionless as a cloud the old Man stood,
That heareth not the loud winds when they call;
And moveth all together, if it move at all.

At length, himself unsettling, he the pond
Stirred with his staff, and fixedly did look
Upon the muddy water, which he conned,
As if he had been reading in a book:
And now a stranger's privilege I took;
And, drawing to his side, to him did say,
'This morning gives us promise of a glorious day.'

A gentle answer did the old Man make,
In courteous speech which forth he slowly drew:
And him with further words I thus bespake,
'What occupation do you there pursue?
This is a lonesome place for one like you.'
Ere he replied, a flash of mild surprise
Broke from the sable orbs of his yet-vivid eyes.

His words came feebly, from a feeble chest,
But each in solemn order followed each,
With something of a lofty utterance drest –
Choice word and measured phrase, above the reach
Of ordinary men; a stately speech;
Such as grave Livers do in Scotland use,
Religious men, who give to God and man their dues.

He told, that to these waters he had come
To gather leeches, being old and poor:
Employment hazardous and wearisome!
And he had many hardships to endure:
From pond to pond he roamed, from moor to moor;
Housing, with God's good help, by choice or chance;
And in this way he gained an honest maintenance.

The old Man still stood talking by my side;
But now his voice to me was like a stream
Scarce heard; nor word from word could I divide;
And the whole body of the Man did seem
Like one whom I had met with in a dream;
Or like a man from some far region sent,
To give me human strength, by apt admonishment.

My former thoughts returned: the fear that kills;
And hope that is unwilling to be fed;
Cold, pain, and labour, and all fleshly ills;
And mighty Poets in their misery dead.
– Perplexed, and longing to be comforted,
My question eagerly did I renew,
'How is it that you live, and what is it you do?'

He with a smile did then his words repeat;
And said that, gathering leeches, far and wide
He travelled; stirring thus about his feet
The waters of the pools where they abide.
'Once I could meet with them on every side;
But they have dwindled long by slow decay;
Yet still I persevere, and find them where I may.'

While he was talking thus, the lonely place,
The old Man's shape, and speech – all troubled me:
In my mind's eye I seemed to see him pace
About the weary moors continually,
Wandering about alone and silently.
While I these thoughts within myself pursued,
He, having made a pause, the same discourse renewed.

And soon with this he other matter blended,
Cheerfully uttered, with demeanour kind,
But stately in the main; and when he ended,
I could have laughed myself to scorn to find
In that decrepit Man so firm a mind.
'God,' said I, 'be my help and stay secure;
I'll think of the Leech-gatherer on the lonely moor!'

PRAYER BEFORE CADIZ

O Lord God, when Thou givest to Thy servants to
endeavour any great matter, grant us to know that it is
not the beginning but the continuing of the same, until
it be thoroughly finished, which yieldeth the true glory.

SIR FRANCIS DRAKE (*c.* 1545–1596)

EPITAPH

God give me work
Till my life shall end
And life
Till my work is done.

WINIFRED HOLTBY (1898–1935)

SEXT

From THE THIRD CENTURY

The Corn was Orient and Immortal Wheat, which never should be reaped, nor was ever sown. I thought it had stood from Everlasting to Everlasting. The Dust and Stones of the Street were as Precious as GOLD. The Gates were at first the End of the World, The Green Trees when I saw them first through one of the Gates Transported and Ravished me; their Sweetnes and unusual Beauty made my Heart to leap, and almost mad with Extasie, they were such strange and Wonderfull Thing[s]: The Men! O what Venerable and Reverend Creatures did the Aged seem! Immortal Cherubims! And yong Men Glittering and Sparkling Angels and Maids strange Seraphick Pieces of Life and Beauty! Boys and Girles Tumbling in the Street, and Playing, were moving Jewels. I knew not that they were Born or should Die. But all things abided Eternaly as they were in their Proper Places. Eternity was Manifest in the Light of the Day, and som thing infinit Behind evry thing appeared: which talked with my Expectation and moved my Desire. The Citie seemed to stand in Eden, or to be Built in Heaven. The Streets were mine, the Temple was mine, the People were mine, their Clothes and Gold and Silver was mine, as much as their Sparkling Eys fair Skins and ruddy faces. The Skies were mine, and so were the Sun and Moon and Stars, and all the World was mine, and I the only Spectator and Enjoyer of it. I knew no Churlish Proprieties, nor Bounds nor Divisions: but all Proprieties and Divisions were mine: all Treasures and the Possessors of them. So that with much adoe I was corrupted; and made to learn the Dirty Devices of this World. Which now I unlearn, and becom as it were a little Child again, that I may enter into the Kingdom of GOD.

THE RETREAT

Happy those early days, when I
Shin'd in my angel-infancy!
Before I understood this place
Appointed for my second race,
Or taught my soul to fancy aught
But a white, celestial thought;
When yet I had not walked above
A mile, or two, from my first love,
And looking back (at that short space)
Could see a glimpse of his bright face;
When on some gilded cloud or flower
My gazing soul would dwell an hour,
And in those weaker glories spy
Some shadows of eternity;
Before I taught my tongue to wound
My conscience with a sinful sound,
Or had the black art to dispense
A several sin to every sense,
But felt through all this fleshly dress
Bright *shoots* of everlastingness.
 O how I long to travel back
And tread again that ancient track!
That I might once more reach that plain
Where first I left my glorious train,
From whence th'Enlightened spirit sees

That shady city of palm-trees;
But (ah!) my soul with too much stay
Is drunk, and staggers in the way.
Some men a forward motion love,
But I by backward steps would move,
And when this dust falls to the urn,
In that state I came, return.

AS KINGFISHERS CATCH FIRE

As kingfishers catch fire, dragonflies draw flame;
    As tumbled over rim in roundy wells
    Stones ring; like each tucked string tells, each hung
        bell's
Bow swung finds tongue to fling out broad its name;
Each mortal thing does one thing and the same:
    Deals out that being indoors each one dwells;
    Selves – goes itself; *myself* it speaks and spells,
Crying *What I do is me: for that I came.*

I say more: the just man justices;
    Keeps gráce: thát keeps all his goings graces;
Acts in God's eye what in God's eye he is –
    Chríst. For Christ plays in ten thousand places,
Lovely in limbs, and lovely in eyes not his
    To the Father through the features of men's faces.

THE WINDHOVER:
To Christ our Lord

I caught this morning morning's minion, king-
   dom of daylight's dauphin, dapple-dawn-drawn
      Falcon, in his riding
   Of the rolling level underneath him steady air, and
      striding
High there, how he rung upon the rein of a wimpling
      wing
In his ecstasy! then off, off forth on swing,
   As a skate's heel sweeps smooth on a bow-bend: the
      hurl and gliding
   Rebuffed the big wind. My heart in hiding
Stirred for a bird, – the achieve of, the mastery of the
      thing!

Brute beauty and valour and act, oh, air, pride, plume,
      here
   Buckle! AND the fire that breaks from thee then, a
      billion
Times told lovelier, more dangerous, O my chevalier!

   No wonder of it: shéer plód makes plough down
      sillion
Shine, and blue-bleak embers, ah my dear,
   Fall, gall themselves, and gash gold-vermilion.

O MOST HIGH, ALMIGHTY,
GOOD LORD GOD

O most high, almighty, good Lord God, to Thee
belong praise, glory, honour and all blessing.

Praised be my Lord God with all his creatures, and
especially our brother the sun, who brings us the day
and who brings us the light; fair is he and shines with a
great splendour; O Lord, he signifies to us Thee.

Praised be my Lord for our sister the moon, and for the
stars, the which he has set clear and lovely in the
heaven.

Praised be my Lord for our sister water, who is very
serviceable unto us and humble and precious and clean.

Praised be my Lord for our brother fire, through whom
Thou givest us light in the darkness; and he is bright
and pleasant and very mighty and strong.

Praised be my Lord for our mother the earth, the
which doth sustain us and keep us, and bringeth forth
divers fruit, and flowers of many colours, and grass.

Praised be my Lord for all those who pardon one another for his love's sake, and who endure weakness and tribulation; blessed are they who peaceably shall endure, for Thou, O most Highest, shalt give them a crown.

Praised be my Lord for our sister the death of the body.

Blessed are they who are found walking by thy most holy will.

Praise ye and bless ye the Lord, and give thanks unto him, and serve him with great humility.

BRAHMAN

There is a light that shines beyond all things on earth,
beyond us all, beyond the heavens, beyond the highest,
the very highest heavens . . .
This is the light that shines in our heart.

All the universe is in truth Brahman. He is the
beginning and end and life of all. As such, in silence,
give unto Him adoration.

There is a spirit that is mind and life, light and truth
and vast spaces. He enfolds the whole universe and in
silence is loving all.

This is the Spirit that is in my heart, smaller than a
grain of mustard seed, greater than the earth, greater
than the heavens, greater than all these worlds.

He contains all work and desires, all perfumes and
tastes.

This is the Spirit in my heart, this is Brahman.

To Him I shall come when I go beyond this life.

And to Him will come he who has faith and doubts not.

CHANDOGYA UPANISHAD (800 BC)   133

SONG OF APOLLO

The sleepless Hours who watch me as I lie
   Curtained with star-enwoven tapestries
From the broad moonlight of the open sky,
   Fanning the busy dreams from my dim eyes, –
Waken me when their mother, the grey Dawn,
Tells them that dreams and that the moon is gone.

Then I arise; and climbing Heaven's blue dome,
   I walk over the mountains and the waves,
Leaving my robe upon the ocean foam;
   My footsteps pave the clouds with fire; the caves
Are filled with my bright presence, and the air
Leaves the green Earth to my embraces bare.

The sunbeams are my shafts with which I kill
   Deceit, that loves the night and fears the day;
All men who do, or even imagine ill
   Fly me; and from the glory of my ray
Good minds and open actions take new might,
Until diminished by the reign of night.

I feed the clouds, the rainbows and the flowers
    With their aethereal colours; the moon's globe
And the pure stars in their eternal bowers
    Are cinctured with my power as with a robe;
Whatever lamps on Earth or Heaven may shine
Are portions of one spirit; which is mine.

I stand at noon upon the peak of Heaven;
    Then with unwilling steps, I linger down
Into the clouds of the Atlantic even;
    For grief that I depart they weep and frown –
What look is more delightful, than the smile
With which I soothe them from the Western isle?

I am the eye with which the Universe
    Beholds itself, and knows it is divine;
All harmony of instrument and verse,
    All prophecy and medicine are mine,
All light of art or nature: – to my song
Victory and praise, in its own right, belong.

PERCY BYSSHE SHELLEY (1792–1822)   135

GOD'S VIRTUE

The world's bright comforter, whose beamsome light
   Poor creatures cheereth, mounting from the deep,
   His course doth in prefixed compass keep;
And, as courageous giant, takes delight
To run his race and exercise his might,
   Till him, down galloping the mountain's steep,
   Clear Hesperus, smooth messenger of sleep,
Views; and the silver ornament of night

Forth brings, with stars past number in her train,
   All which with sun's long borrowed splendour shine.
The seas, with full tide swelling, ebb again;
   All years to their old quarters new resign;
     The winds forsake their mountain-chambers wild,
     And all in all things with God's virtue filled.

LORD, ENFOLD ME

Lord, enfold me in the depths of your heart; and there
hold me, refine, purge, and set me on fire, raise me
aloft, until my own self knows utter annihilation.

TEILHARD DE CHARDIN (1881–1955)
TRANS. BERNARD WALL

WONDERFUL TO COME OUT LIVING

Wonderful to come out living
   From the fiery furnace-blast,
But yet more, that after testing
   I shall be fine gold at last;
Time of cleansing! Time of winnowing!
   Yet 'tis calm, without dismay;
He who soon shall be my refuge
   Holds the winnowing-fan today.

ANN GRIFFITHS (1776–1805)

SPLENDIDIS LONGUM VALEDICO NUGIS

Leave me, O Love, which reaches but to dust;
  And thou, my mind, aspire to higher things;
Grow rich in that which never taketh rust;
  Whatever fades but fading pleasure brings.
Draw in thy beams, and humble all thy might
  To that sweet yoke where lasting freedoms be;
Which breaks the clouds and opens forth the light,
  That doth both shine and give us sight to see.
O take fast hold; let that light be thy guide
  In this small course which birth draws out to death,
And think how evil becometh him to slide,
  Who seeketh heaven, and comes of heavenly breath.
    Then farewell, world; thy uttermost I see;
    Eternal Love, maintain thy life in me.

VENI CREATOR SPIRITUS

Creator Spirit, by whose aid
The world's foundations first were laid,
Come visit ev'ry pious mind;
Come pour thy joys on human kind:
From sin, and sorrow set us free;
And make thy temples worthy thee.

O, source of uncreated light,
The Father's promis'd *Paraclete*!
Thrice holy fount, thrice holy fire,
Our hearts with heav'nly love inspire;
Come, and thy sacred unction bring
To sanctifie us, while we sing!

Plenteous of grace, descend from high,
Rich in thy sev'n-fold energy!
Thou strength of his almighty hand,
Whose pow'r does heav'n and earth command:
Proceeding Spirit, our defence,
Who do'st the gift of tongues dispence,
And crown'st thy gift, with eloquence!

Refine and purge our earthy parts;
But, oh, inflame and fire our hearts!
Our frailties help, our vice controul;
Submit the senses to the soul;
And when rebellious they are grown,
Then, lay thy hand, and hold 'em down.

Chace from our minds th' infernal foe;
And Peace, the fruit of love, bestow:
And, lest our feet shou'd step astray,
Protect, and guide us in the way.

Make us eternal truths receive,
And practise, all that we believe:
Give us thy self, that we may see
The Father and the Son, by thee.

Immortal honour, endless fame
Attend th'almighty Father's name:
The saviour Son, be glorify'd,
Who for lost man's redemption dy'd:
And equal adoration be
Eternal *Paraclete*, to thee.

FIRE OF THE SPIRIT

Fire of the Spirit, life of the lives of creatures,
spiral of sanctity, bond of all natures,
glow of charity, lights of clarity, taste
of sweetness to sinners, be with us and hear us . . .

Composer of all things, light of all the risen,
key of salvation, release from the dark prison,
hope of all unions, scope of chastities, joy
in the glory, strong honour, be with us and hear us.

ST HILDEGARDE (12TH CENTURY),
TRANS. CHARLES WILLIAMS

MY PRAYERS MUST MEET A BRAZEN HEAVEN

My prayers must meet a brazen heaven
And fail or scatter all away.
Unclean and seeming unforgiven
My prayers I scarcely call to pray.
I cannot buoy my heart above;
Above it cannot entrance win.
I reckon precedents of love,
But feel the long success of sin.

My heaven is brass and iron my earth:
Yea iron is mingled with my clay,
So harden'd is it in this dearth
Which praying fails to do away.
Nor tears nor tears this clay uncouth
Could mould, if any tears there were.
A warfare of my lips in truth,
Battling with God, is now my prayer.

MY SPIRIT LONGS FOR THEE

My spirit longs for Thee
   Within my troubled breast,
Though I unworthy be
   Of so divine a Guest.

Of so divine a Guest
   Unworthy though I be,
Yet has my heart no rest
   Unless it come from Thee.

Unless it come from Thee,
   In vain I look around;
In all that I can see
   No rest is to be found.

No rest is to be found
   But in Thy blessèd love:
O, let my wish be crowned,
   And send it from above!

J. BYROM (1692–1763)

PRAISE BE TO HIM WHO ALONE
IS TO BE PRAISED

Praise be to him who alone is to be praised. Praise him
for his grace and favour. Praise him for his power and
goodness. Praise him whose knowledge encompasses
all things.

O God, grant me light in my heart and light in my
tomb, light in my hearing and light in my seeing, light
in my flesh, light in my blood and light in my bones.

Light before me, light behind me, light to right of me,
light to left of me, light above me, light beneath me.

O God, increase my light and give me the greatest
light of all. Of thy mercy grant me light, O thou most
merciful.

ASCENSION HYMN

They are all gone into the world of light!
    And I alone sit lingering here.
Their very memory is fair and bright,
    And my sad thoughts doth clear.

It glows and glitters in my cloudy breast
    Like stars upon some gloomy grove,
Or those faint beams in which this hill is drest
    After the sun's remove.

I see them walking in an air of glory
    Whose light doth trample on my days;
My days, which are at best but dull and hoary,
    Mere glimmering and decays.

O holy hope! and high humility,
    High as the Heavens above!
These are your walks, and you have shew'd them me
    To kindle my cold love,

Dear, beauteous death! the jewel of the just,
    Shining nowhere but in the dark,
What mysteries do lie beyond thy dust,
    Could man outlook that mark!

He that hath found some fledged bird's nest, may know
   At first sight if the bird be flown;
But what fair well or grove he sings in now,
   That is to him unknown.

And yet, as angels in some brighter dreams
   Call to the soul, when man doth sleep,
So some strange thoughts transcend our wonted
      themes,
   And into glory peep.

If a star were confin'd into a tomb
   Her captive flames must needs burn there;
But when the hand that locked her up, gives room,
   She'll shine through all the sphere.

O Father of eternal life, and all
   Created glories under thee!
Resume thy spirit from this world of thrall
   Into true liberty.

Either disperse these mists, which blot and fill
   My perspective (still) as they pass,
Or else remove me hence unto that hill
   Where I shall need no glass.

ALL CREATURES OF OUR GOD AND KING

All creatures of our God and King,
Lift up your voice and with us sing
    Alleluia, Alleluia!
Thou burning sun with golden beam,
Thou silver moon with softer gleam,
     O praise him, O praise him,
     Alleluia, Alleluia, Alleluia!

Thou rushing wind that art so strong,
Ye clouds that sail in heaven along,
    O praise him, Alleluia!
Thou rising morn, in praise rejoice,
Ye lights of evening, find a voice:

Thou flowing water, pure and clear,
Make music for thy Lord to hear,
    Alleluia, Alleluia!
Thou fire so masterful and bright,
That givest man both warmth and light:

Dear mother earth, who day by day
Unfoldest blessings on our way,
    O praise him, Alleluia!
The flowers and fruits that in thee grow,
Let them his glory also show:

And all ye men of tender heart,
Forgiving others, take your part,
    O sing ye, Alleluia!
Ye who long pain and sorrow bear,
Praise God and on him cast your care:

And thou most kind and gentle Death,
Waiting to hush our latest breath,
    O praise him, Alleluia!
Thou leadest home the child of God,
And Christ our Lord the way hath trod:

Let all things their Creator bless,
And worship him in humbleness,
    O praise him, Alleluia!
Praise, praise the Father, praise the Son,
And praise the Spirit, Three in One:

NONES

From THE FIRST CENTURY

What is more Easy and Sweet then Meditation? yet in this hath God commended his Lov, that by Meditation it is Enjoyed. As Nothing is more Easy then to Think, so nothing is more Difficult then to Think Well. The Easiness of Thinking we received from God, the Difficulty of thinking Well, proceedeth from our selvs. Yet in Truth, it is far more Easy to think well then Ill, becaus Good Thoughts be sweet and Delightfull: Evil Thoughts are full of Discontent and Trouble. So that an Evil Habit, and Custom hav made it Difficult to think well, not Nature. For by Nature, nothing is so Difficult as to Think amiss.

THOMAS TRAHERNE (1637–1674)   151

From THE CLOUD OF UNKNOWING

Nevertheless, there are helps which the apprentice in contemplation should employ, namely, Lesson, Meditation, and Orison, or, as they are more generally called, Reading, Thinking, and Praying. These three are dealt with elsewhere by another writer much better than I could deal with them, and I need not, therefore, tell you here about them. Except to say this: these three are so interwoven, that for beginners and proficients – but not for the perfect (we mean on the human level) – thinking may not be had unless reading or hearing come first. It is the same for all: clergy read books, and the man in the street 'reads' the clergy when he hears them preach the word of God. Beginners and proficients cannot pray unless they think first.

Prove it: God's word, written or spoken, can be likened to a mirror. Spiritually, the 'eye' of your soul is your reason: your conscience is your spiritual 'face'. Just as you cannot see or know that there is a dirty mark on your actual face without the aid of a mirror, or somebody telling you, so spiritually, it is impossible for a soul blinded by his frequent sins to see the dirty mark in his conscience, without reading or hearing God's word.

It follows that if a man sees where the dirty mark is on his face, either in a mirror or because someone has told him – true spiritually as well as literally – then, and not till then, he runs off to the well to wash himself. If the dirty mark is deliberate sin, the 'well' is Holy Church, and the 'water' confession, and all that goes with it. If it is a sin deeply rooted, and productive of evil impulses, then the 'well' is all-merciful God, and the 'water' prayer, and all that that involves. Thus we see that beginners and proficients cannot think unless they read or hear first, and they cannot pray without prior thinking.

But this is not the case with those who practise contemplation, that is, the readers of this book. Meditation for them is, as it were, the sudden recognition and groping awareness of their own wretchedness, or God's goodness. There has been no prior help from reading or sermons, no special meditation on anything whatever. This sudden perception and awareness is better learned from God than man. I do not mind at all if you, at this stage, have no other meditations upon your own wretchedness, or upon God's goodness (obviously I am assuming that you are moved by the grace of God in this matter, and are under direction), than such as come through the single word SIN or GOD, or some suchlike word of your own choosing. Do not analyse or expound these words with imaginative cleverness, as if, by considering their constituent parts, you would increase your devotion. I do not believe you should ever attempt

153

this in the time of contemplation. But take the words as they are, whole. Mean by 'sin' the whole lump of it, not particularizing about any part, for it is nothing other than yourself. I think that this almost instinctive awareness of sin, which you have solidified into a lump, and which is nothing but yourself, should make you the maddest person on earth, needing restraint! But no one looking at you would guess it from your appearance: sober in habit, giving nothing away by your expression, and doing whatever it is, sitting, walking, lying down, relaxing, standing, kneeling, in perfect calm!

ANON. (14TH CENTURY),
TRANS. CLIFTON WOLTERS

From THE BREWING OF SOMA

Dear Lord and Father of mankind,
    Forgive our foolish ways!
Reclothe us in our rightful mind,
In purer lives thy service find,
    In deeper reverence, praise.

In simple trust like theirs who heard
    Beside the Syrian sea
The gracious calling of the Lord,
Let us, like them, without a word,
    Rise up and follow thee.

O Sabbath rest by Galilee!
    O calm of hills above,
Where Jesus knelt to share with thee
The silence of eternity
    Interpreted by love!

With that deep hush subduing all
    Our words and works that drown
The tender whisper of thy call,
As noiseless let thy blessing fall
    As fell thy manna down.

Drop thy still dews of quietness,
    Till all our strivings cease;
Take from our souls the strain and stress,
And let our ordered lives confess
    The beauty of thy peace.

Breathe through the heats of our desire
    Thy coolness and thy balm;
Let sense be dumb, let flesh retire;
Speak through the earthquake, wind, and fire,
    O still, small voice of calm!

I'LL HOPE NO MORE

I'll hope no more
For things that will not come;
And, if they do, they prove but cumbersome;
    Wealth brings much woe:
    And, since it fortunes so,
    'Tis better to be poor,
    Than so t'abound,
    As to be drownd,
Or overwhelm'd with store.

Pale care, avant,
I'll learn to be content
With that small stock, Thy bounty gave or lent.
    What may conduce
    To my most healthful use,
    Almighty God, me grant;
    But that, or this,
    That hurtful is
Deny Thy suppliant.

ROBERT HERRICK (1591–1674)

OF THE PRESENCE OF GOD

The soul that is faithful in the exercise of love and adherence to GOD above described, is astonished to feel Him gradually taking possession of their whole being: it now enjoys a continual sense of that Presence, which is become as it were natural to it; and this, as well as prayer, is the result of habit. The soul feels an unusual serenity gradually being diffused throughout all its faculties; and silence now wholly constitutes its prayer; whilst GOD communicates an intuitive love, which is the beginning of ineffable blessedness.

We must, however, urge it as a matter of the highest import, to cease from self-action and self-exertion, that GOD Himself may act alone: He saith, by the mouth of His Prophet David, '*Be still, and know that I am God*' (*Ps.* xlvi. 10). But the creature is so infatuated with a love and attachment to its own workings, that it imagines nothing at all is done, if it doth not perceive and distinguish all its operations. It is ignorant that its inability minutely to observe the manner of its motion is occasioned by the swiftness of its progress; and that the operations of GOD, in extending and diffusing their influence, absorb those of the creature. The stars may be seen distinctly before the sun rises; but as his light advances, their rays are gradually absorbed by his and they become invisible, not from the want of light in themselves, but from the superior effulgence of the chief luminary.

The case is similar here; for there is a strong and universal light which absorbs all the little distinct lights of the soul; they grow faint and disappear under its powerful influence, and self-activity is now no longer distinguishable: yet those greatly err who accuse this prayer of idleness, a charge that can arise only from inexperience. If they would but make some efforts towards the attainment of this prayer, they would soon experience the contrary of what they suppose and find their accusation groundless.

This appearance of inaction is, indeed, not the consequence of sterility and want, but of fruitfulness and abundance which will be clearly perceived by the experienced soul, who will know and feel that the silence is full and unctuous, and the result of causes totally the reverse of apathy and barrenness. There are two kinds of people that keep silence; the one because they have nothing to say, the other because they have too much: it is so with the soul in this state; the silence is occasioned by the superabundance of matter, too great for utterance.

To be drowned, and to die of thirst, are deaths widely different; yet water may, in some sense, be said to cause both; abundance destroys in one case, and want in the other. So in this state the abundance and overflowings of grace still the activity of self; and, therefore, it is of the utmost importance to remain as silent as possible.

The infant hanging at the mother's breast is a lively illustration of our subject: it begins to draw the milk by moving its little lips; but when the milk flows abundantly, it is content to swallow, and suspends its suction: by doing otherwise it would only hurt itself, spill the milk and be obliged to quit the breast.

We must act in like manner in the beginning of Prayer, by exerting the lips of the affections; but as soon as the milk of Divine Grace flows freely, we have nothing to do but, in repose and stillness, sweetly to imbibe it; and when it ceases to flow, we must again stir up the affections as the infant moves its lips. Whoever acts otherwise cannot turn this grace to advantage, which is bestowed to allure and draw the soul into the repose of Love, and not into the multiplicity of Self.

But what becometh of this child, who gently and without motion drinketh in the milk? Who would believe that it can thus receive nourishment? Yet the more peacefully it feeds, the better it thrives. What, I say, becomes of this infant? It drops gently asleep on its mother's bosom. So the soul that is tranquil and peaceful in prayer, sinketh frequently into a mystic slumber, wherein all its powers are at rest; till at length it is wholly fitted for that state, of which it enjoys these transient anticipations. In this process the soul is led naturally, without effort, art, or study.

The Interior is not a stronghold to be taken by storm and violence, but a kingdom of peace, which is to be gained only by love.

If any will thus pursue the little path I have pointed out, it will lead them to intuitive prayer. God demands nothing extraordinary nor difficult; on the contrary, He is best pleased by a simple and child-like conduct.

That which is most sublime and elevated in religion is the easiest attained: the most necessary Sacraments are the least difficult. It is thus also in natural things: if you would go to sea, embark on a river, and you will be conveyed to it insensibly and without exertion. Would you go to God, follow this sweet and simple path, and you will arrive at the desired object, with an ease and expedition that will amaze you.

The soul advanced thus far hath no need of any other preparation than its quietude: for now the Presence of God, which is the great effect, or rather continuation of Prayer, begins to be infused, and almost without intermission. The soul enjoys transcendent blessedness, and feels that 'it no longer lives, but that Christ liveth in it'; and that the only way to find Him is introversion. No sooner do the bodily eyes close than the soul is wrapt up in Prayer: it is amazed at so great a blessing, and enjoys an internal converse, which external matters cannot interrupt.

MADAME GUYON (1648–1717),   161
TRANS. ANON.

LORD, FOR THE ERRING THOUGHT

Lord, for the erring thought
Not into evil wrought:
Lord, for the wicked will
Betrayed and baffled still:
For the heart from itself kept,
Our thanksgiving accept.

For ignorant hopes that were
Broken to our blind prayer:
For pain, death, sorrow, sent
Unto our chastisement:
For all loss of seeming good,
Quicken our gratitude.

THE SONG OF BLESSING

Not to serve the foolish, but to serve the wise,
To honour those worthy of honour – this is the highest
    blessing.

Much insight and education, self-control and pleasant
    speech,
And whatever word be well-spoken – this is the
    highest blessing.

Service to mother and father, the company of wife and
    child,
And peaceful pursuits – this is the highest blessing.

Almsgiving and righteousness, the company of
    kinsfolk,
Blameless works – this is the highest blessing.

To dwell in a pleasant land, with right desire in the
    heart,
To bear remembrance of good deeds – this is the
    highest blessing.

Reverence and humility, cheerfulness and gratitude,
    listening in due season to the Dhamma – this is
    the highest blessing.

Self-control and virtue, vision of the Noble Truths,
And winning to Nirvana – this is the highest blessing.

Beneath the stroke of life's changes, the mind that does
    not shake
But abides without grief or passion – this is the highest
    blessing.

On every side invincible are they who do thus,
They come to salvation – theirs is the highest blessing.

DO YOU SEEK NO MORE OF HIM

Do you seek no more of Him than to name His Name?

We are the flute: our music is all Thine.

The sun of the soul sets not and has no yesterday.

Love is the astrolabe of God's mysteries.

If the sun that illumines the world were to draw nearer,
The world would be consumed.

God has chosen me to be His house.

If thou takest umbrage at every rub
How wilt thou become a polished mirror?

O God, show us all things in this house of deception:
Show them all as they really are.

Through love the stake becomes a throne,
Through love the king becomes a slave.

Our soul, the breath of our praise, steals away
Little by little from the prison of this world ...
Our breaths soar up with choice words, as a gift from us

To the abode of everlastingness.
Then comes to us the recompense of our praise,
A recompense manifold from God the merciful.
Then He causes us to seek more good words, so that
His servant may win more of His mercy.
Verily the source of our delight in prayer
Is the divine Love which without rest
Draws the soul home.

THE WILL OF GOD

One goodness ruleth by its single will
All things that are, and have been, and shall be,
Itself abiding, knowing naught of change.
This is true health, this is the blessed life.
Here, O ye prisoners of empty hope,
Minds kept in bonds by pleasure, haste ye to return.
Here, here your rest, sure rest for all your hurt,
Eternal harbour for your quiet anchorage,
Shelter and refuge for unhappy men
That's always open.
This is the Father, and the Son, and the kind Holy
    Ghost,
One King omnipotent, one called the Trinity.
One love, O thou that readest, that shall be
Thine to eternity,
That sent this mighty gift of books
That reading, thou mightst recognize thy Maker,
King, Maker of all things, Father, Redeemer,
The Saviour Christ, to whom be glory.

ALCUIN OF YORK (735–804),
TRANS. HELEN WADDELL

THE UNCHANGEABLENESS OF GOD

If we human beings are mere shadows, as is sometimes said, He is eternal clearness in eternal unchangeableness. If we are shadows that glide away – my soul, look well to thyself; for whether you will it or not, you go to meet eternity, to meet Him, and He is eternal clearness. Hence it is not so much that He keeps a reckoning, as that He is Himself the reckoning. It is said that we must render up an account, as if we perhaps had a long time to prepare for it, and also perhaps as if it were likely to be cluttered up with such an enormous mass of detail as to make it impossible to get the reckoning finished: O my soul, the account is every moment complete! For the unchangeable clearness of God is the reckoning, complete to the last detail, preserved by Him who is eternally unchangeable, and who has forgotten nothing of the things that I have forgotten, and who does not, as I do, remember some things otherwise than they really were.

There is thus sheer fear and trembling in this thought of the unchangeableness of God, almost as if it were far, far beyond the power of any human being to sustain a relationship to such an unchangeable power; aye, as if this thought must drive a man to such unrest and anxiety of mind as to bring him to the verge of despair.

But then it is also true that *there is rest and happiness in this thought.* It is really true that when, wearied with all this human inconstancy, this temporal and earthly mutability, and wearied also of your own inconstancy, you might wish to find a place where rest may be found for your weary head, your weary thoughts, your weary spirit, so that you might rest and find complete repose: Oh, in the unchangeableness of God there is rest! When you therefore permit this unchangeableness to serve you according to His will, for your own welfare, your eternal welfare; when you submit yourself to discipline, so that your selfish will (and it is from this that the change chiefly comes, more than from the outside) dies away, the sooner the better – and there is no help for it, you must whether willing or resisting, for think how vain it is for your will to be at odds with an eternal immutability; be therefore as the child when it profoundly feels that it has over against itself a will in relation to which nothing avails except obedience – when you submit to be disciplined by His unchangeable will, so as to renounce inconstancy and changeableness and caprice and self-will: then you will steadily rest more and more securely, and more and more blessedly, in the unchangeableness of God. For that the thought of God's unchangeableness is a blessed thought – who can doubt it? But take heed that you become of such a mind that you can rest happily in this immutability! Oh, as one is wont to speak who has a happy home, so speaks such an individual. He says: my home is eternally secure, I rest in the unchangeableness of God. This is a rest that no one can disturb for you except yourself; if you could become completely obedient in invariable obedience, you would each and every moment, with the same necessity as that by which a heavy body sinks to the earth or a light body moves upward, freely rest in God.

170   SØREN KIERKEGAARD (1813–1855),
TRANS. D. SWENSON

THE HABIT OF PERFECTION

Elected Silence, sing to me
And beat upon my whorlèd ear,
Pipe me to pastures still and be
The music that I care to hear.

Shape nothing, lips; be lovely-dumb:
It is the shut, the curfew sent
From there where all surrenders come
Which only makes you eloquent.

Be shellèd, eyes, with double dark
And find the uncreated light:
This ruck and reel which you remark
Coils, keeps, and teases simple sight.

Palate, the hutch of tasty lust,
Desire not to be rinsed with wine:
The can must be so sweet, the crust
So fresh that come in fasts divine!

Nostrils, your careless breath that spend
Upon the stir and keep of pride,
What relish shall the censers send
Along the sanctuary side!

O feel-of-primrose hands, O feet
That want the yield of plushy sward,
But you shall walk the golden street
And you unhouse and house the Lord.

And, Poverty, be thou the bride
And now the marriage feast begun,
And lily-covered clothes provide
Your spouse not laboured-at nor spun.

IT IS GOOD TO BE HAPPY ALONE

One great Discouragement to Felicity, or rather to great Souls in the persuit of Felicity, is the Solitariness of the Way that leadeth to her Temple. A man that studies Happiness must sit alone like a Sparrow upon the Hous Top, and like a Pelican in the Wilderness. And the reason is becaus all men prais Happiness and despise it · very few shall a Man find in the way of Wisdom: And few indeed that having given up their Names to Wisdom and felicity, that will persevere in seeking it. Either He must go on alone, or go back for company. People are tickled with the Name of it, and som are persuaded to Enterprize a little, but quickly draw back when they see the trouble, yea cool of them selvs without any Trouble. Those Mysteries which while men are Ignorant of, they would giv all the Gold in the World for, I hav seen when Known to be despised. Not as if the Nature of Happiness were such that it did need a vail: but the Nature of Man is such, that it is Odious and ingratefull. For those things which are most Glorious when most Naked, are by Men when most Nakedly reveald most Despised. So that GOD is fain for His very Names sake, lest His Beauties should be scorned to conceal her Beauties: and for the sake of Men, which naturaly are more prone to prie into secret and forbidden things then into Open and common. Felicity is amiable under a Vail, but most Amiable when most Naked. It hath its times, and seasons for both. There is som Pleasure in breaking the Shell: and many Delights in our Addresses, previous to the Sweets in the Possession of her. It is som Part of Felicity that we must seek her.

In order to this, he furnished him self with this Maxime. *It is a Good Thing to be Happy alone.* It is better to be Happy in Company, but Good to be Happy alone. Men owe me the Advantage of their Society, but if they deny me that just Debt, I will not be unjust to my self, and side with them in bereaving me. I will not be Discouraged, least I be Miserable for Company. More Company increases Happiness, but does not leighten or Diminish Misery.

In Order to Interior or Contemplativ Happiness, it is a Good Principle: that Apprehensions within are better then their Objects. Morneys Simile of the Saw is admirable. If a man would cut with a saw, he must not apprehend it to be a Knife, but a Thing with Teeth; otherwise he cannot use it. He that mistakes his Knife to be an Auger, or his Hand to be his Meat, confounds him self by misapplications. These Mistakes are Ocular · but far more Absurd ones are unseen. To mistake the World, or the Nature of ones soul, is a more Dangerous Error. He that Thinks the Heavens and the Earth not his, can hardly use them: he that thinks the Sons of Men impertinent to his Joy and Happiness can scarcely lov them. But he that Knows them to be Instruments and what they are will delight in them, and is able to use them. Whatever we misapprehend we cannot use. Nor well enjoy, what we cannot use. Nor can a thing be our Happines, we cannot enjoy. Nothing therfore can be our Happiness, but that alone which we rightly apprehend. To apprehend God our Enemie destroys our Happiness. Inward Apprehensions are the very light of Blessednes, and the Cement of Souls and their Objects.

I ASKED FOR PEACE

I asked for Peace –
My sins arose,
And bound me close,
I could not find release.

I asked for Truth –
My doubts came in,
And with their din
They wearied all my youth.

I asked for Love –
My lovers failed,
And griefs assailed
Around, beneath, above.

I asked for Thee –
And Thou didst come
To take me home
Within Thy heart to be.

From HIS PILGRIMAGE

Give me my scallop-shell of quiet,
My staff of faith to walk upon,
My scrip of joy, immortal diet,
My bottle of salvation,
My gown of Glory, hope's true gage;
And thus I'll take my pilgrimage.

PEACE

Sweet Peace, where dost thou dwell? I humbly crave,
                  Let me once know.
        I sought thee in a secret cave,
        And ask'd, if Peace were there.
A hollow wind did seem to answer, No:
                  Go seek elsewhere.

I did; and going did a rainbow note:
                  Surely, thought I,
        This is the lace of Peace's coat:
        I will search out the matter.
But while I look't, the clouds immediately
                  Did break and scatter.

Then went I to a garden, and did spy
                  A gallant flower,
        The crown Imperial: Sure, said I,
        Peace at the root must dwell.
But when I digg'd, I saw a worm devour
                  What show'd so well.

At length I met a rev'rend good old man,
                    Whom when for Peace
          I did demand; he thus began:
          There was a Prince of old
At Salem dwelt, who liv'd with good increase
                    Of flock and fold.

He sweetly liv'd; yet sweetness did not save
                    His life from foes.
          But after death out of his grave
          There sprang twelve stalks of wheat:
Which many wondring at, got some of those
                    To plant and set.

It prosper'd strangely, and did soon disperse
                    Through all the earth:
          For they that taste it do rehearse
          That virtue lies therein,
A secret virtue bringing peace and mirth
                    By flight of sin.

Take of this grain, which in my garden grows,
                    And grows for you;
          Make bread of it: and that repose
          And peace which ev'ry where
With so much earnestness you do pursue,
                    Is only there.

GEORGE HERBERT (1593–1633)   179

MAY THERE BE PEACE

May there be peace in the higher regions; may there be peace in the firmament; may there be peace on earth. May the waters flow peacefully; may the herbs and plants grow peacefully; may all the divine powers bring unto us peace. The supreme Lord is peace. May we all be in peace, peace, and only peace; and may that peace come unto each of us.

Shanti [Peace] – *Shanti* – *Shanti!*

LOOK HOME

Retirèd thoughts enjoy their own delights,
As beauty doth, in self-beholding eye;
Man's mind a mirror is, of heavenly sights,
A brief, wherein all marvels summèd lie;
Of fairest forms and sweetest shapes the store,
Most graceful all, yet thought may grace them more.

The mind a creature is, yet can create,
To nature's patterns adding higher skill;
Of finest works, wit better could the state
If force of wit had equal power of will;
Devise of man in working hath no end;
What thought can think, another thought can mend.

Man's soul, of endless beauties image is,
Drawn by the work of endless skill and might;
This skilful might gave many sparks of bliss,
And to discern this bliss a native light.
To frame God's image as his worths required,
His might, his skill, his word, and will conspired.

All that he had, his image should present;
All that it should present, he could afford;
To that he could afford, his will was bent,
His will was followed with performing word.
Let this suffice, by this conceive the rest:
He should, he could, he would, he did the best.

PEACE

My soul, there is a country
   Far beyond the stars,
Where stands a wingèd sentry
   All skilful in the wars.
There, above noise and danger,
   Sweet peace sits crown'd with smiles,
And one born in a manger
   Commands the beauteous files.
He is thy gracious friend
   And (O my soul, awake!)
Did in pure love descend
   To die here for thy sake.
If thou canst get but thither,
   There grows the flower of peace,
The rose that cannot wither,
   Thy fortress, and thy ease.
Leave then thy foolish ranges;
   For none can thee secure
But one, who never changes,
   Thy God, thy life, thy cure.

HENRY VAUGHAN (1621–1695)

WHEREVER I WENT

Wherever I went I met words and did not understand them.

A lump of doubt inside the mind was like a willow-basket.

For three years, residing in the woods by the stream, I was altogether unhappy.

When unexpectedly I happened to meet the Dharma-raja [Ch'an Master] sitting on a rug.

I advanced towards him, earnestly desiring him to dissolve my doubt.

The master rose from the rug on which he sat deeply absorbed in meditation:

Then, baring his arm, he gave me a blow with his fist on my chest.

This all of a sudden exploded my lump of doubt completely in pieces.

Raising my head, I perceived for the first time that the sun was circular.

Since then I have been the happiest man in the world, with no fears, no worries.

Day in day out I pass my time in a most lively way.

Only I notice my inside filled with a sense of fullness and satisfaction.

I do not go out any longer, hither and thither, with my begging bowl for food.

LOHAN HOSHANG OF SHŌSHU,
  TRANS. D. T. SUZUKI

ROADS TO ENLIGHTENMENT

Beloved Pan, and all ye other gods who haunt this place,
give me beauty in the inward soul; and may the outward
and inward man be at one. May I reckon the wise to be
the wealthy, and may I have such a quantity of gold as a
temperate man and he only can bear and carry –
Anything more? This prayer, I think, is enough for me.

SOCRATES (469–399 BC),
TRANS. BENJAMIN JOWETT

There are three different paths to reach the Highest:
The path of I, the path of Thou and the path of Thou
        and I.
According to the first, all that is, was, or ever shall be
is I, my higher Self. In other words, I am, I was, and I
shall be for ever in Eternity.
According to the second, Thou art, O Lord, and all is
        Thine.
And according to the third, Thou art the Lord, and I
        am Thy servant, or Thy son.

RAMAKRISHNA (1834–1886)   185
TRANS. SWAMI NIKHILANANDA

VESPERS

THE MOON

The Moon's the same old moon
The flowers exactly as they were
Yet I've become the thingness
Of all the things I see.

BUNAN (17TH CENTURY),
TRANS. LUCIEN STRYK

CLOUD STREET

I moved across the Dharma-nature
The earth was buoyant, marvellous,
That very night, whipping its iron horse,
The void galloped into Cloud Street.

GETSUDO (13TH CENTURY),
TRANS. LUCIEN STRYK

HURRAHING IN HARVEST

Summer ends now; now, barbarous in beauty, the
      stooks rise
Around; up above, what wind-walks! what lovely
      behaviour
Of silk-sack clouds! has wilder, wilful-wavier
Meal-drift moulded ever and melted across skies?

I walk, I lift up, I lift up heart, eyes,
Down all that glory in the heavens to glean our
      Saviour;
And, éyes, heárt, what looks, what lips yet gave you a
Rapturous love's greeting of realer, of rounder replies?

And the azurous hung hills are his world-wielding
      shoulder
Majestic – as a stallion stalwart, very-violet-sweet! –
These things, these things were here and but the
      beholder
Wanting; which two when they once meet,
The heart rears wings bold and bolder
And hurls for him, O half hurls earth for him off under
      his feet.

Tuesday, 14 March, 1871

The afternoon had been stormy but it cleared towards sunset. Gradually the heavy rain clouds rolled across the valley to the foot of the opposite mountains and began climbing up their sides wreathing in rolling masses of vapour. One solitary cloud still hung over the brilliant sunlit town, and that whole cloud was a rainbow. Gradually it lost its bright prismatic hues and moved away up the Cusop Dingle in the shape of a pillar and of the colour of golden dark smoke. The Black Mountains were invisible, being wrapped in clouds, and I saw one very white brilliant dazzling cloud where the mountains ought to have been. This cloud grew more white and dazzling every moment, till a clearer burst of sunlight scattered the mists and revealed the truth. This brilliant white cloud that I had been looking and wondering at was the mountain in snow. The last cloud and mist rolled away over the mountain tops and the mountains stood up in the clear blue heaven, a long rampart line of dazzling glittering snow so as no fuller on earth can white them. I stood rooted to the ground, struck with amazement and overwhelmed at the extra-ordinary splendour of this marvellous spectacle. I never saw anything to equal it I think, even among the high Alps. One's first involuntary thought in the presence of these magnificent sights is to lift up the heart to God and humbly thank Him for having made the earth so beautiful. An intense glare of primrose light streamed from the west deepening into rose and crimson. There was not a flake of snow anywhere but on the mountains and they stood up, the great white range rising high into the blue sky, while all the rest of the world at their feet lay ruddy rosy brown. The sudden contrast was tremendous, electrifying. I could have cried with the excitement of the overwhelming spectacle. I wanted someone to admire the sight with me. A man came whistling along the road riding upon a cart horse. I would have stopped him and drawn his attention to the mountains but I thought he would probably consider me mad. He did not seem to be the least struck by or to be taking the smallest notice of the great sight. But it seemed to me as if one might never see such a sight again. The great white range which had at first gleamed with an intense brilliant yellow light gradually deepened with the sky to the indescribable red tinge that snow-fields assume in sunset light, and then the grey cold tint crept up the great slopes quenching the rosy warmth which lingered still a few minutes on the summits. Soon all was cold and grey and all that was left of the brilliant gleaming range was the dim ghostly phantom of the mountain rampart scarce distinguishable from the greying sky.

192   FRANCIS KILVERT (1840–1879)

MY OWN HEART LET ME MORE
HAVE PITY ON

My own heart let me more have pity on; let
Me live to my sad self hereafter kind,
Charitable; not live this tormented mind
With this tormented mind tormenting yet.

I cast for comfort I can no more get
By groping round my comfortless, than blind
Eyes in their dark can day or thirst can find
Thirst's all-in-all in all a world of wet.

Soul, self; come, poor Jackself, I do advise
You, jaded, let be; call off thoughts awhile
Elsewhere; leave comfort root-room; let joy size

At God knows when to God knows what; whose smile
's not wrung, see you; unforeseen times rather – as
        skies
Betweenpie mountains – lights a lovely mile.

GERARD MANLEY HOPKINS (1844–1889)

WHEN THE HEART IS HARD

When the heart is hard and parched up, come upon me
    with a shower of mercy.
When grace is lost from life, come with a burst of song.
When tumultuous work raises its din on all sides
    shutting me out from beyond, come to me, my
    lord of silence, with thy peace and rest.
When my beggarly heart sits crouched, shut up in a
    corner, break open the door, my king, and come
    with the ceremony of a king.
When desire blinds the mind with delusion and dust, O
    thou holy one, thou wakeful, come with thy light
    and thy thunder.

THE KADDISH

Let us magnify and let us sanctify the great name of God in the world which He created according to His will. May His kingdom come in your lifetime, and in your days, and in the lifetime of the family of Israel – quickly and speedily may it come. Amen.

May the greatness of His being be blessed from eternity to eternity.

Let us bless and let us extol, let us tell aloud and let us raise aloft, let us set on high and let us honour, let us exalt and let us praise the Holy One – blessed be He! – though He is far beyond any blessing or song, any honour or any consolation that can be spoken of in this world. Amen.

May great peace from heaven and the gift of life be granted to us and to all the family of Israel. Amen.

May He who makes peace in the highest bring this peace upon us and upon all Israel. Amen.

TRANS. THE REFORM SYNAGOGUES OF GREAT BRITAIN (DATE UNKNOWN)

ST DENIS'S PRAYER

You are wisdom, uncreated and eternal,
    the supreme first cause, above all being,
    sovereign Godhead, sovereign goodness,
    watching unseen the God-inspired wisdom of
        Christian people.
Raise us, we pray, that we may totally respond
    to the supreme, unknown, ultimate, and splendid
        height
of your words, mysterious and inspired.
There all God's secret matters lie covered and hidden
    under darkness both profound and brilliant, silent
        and wise.

You make what is ultimate and beyond brightness
    secretly to shine in all that is most dark.
In your way, ever unseen and intangible,
    you fill to the full with most beautiful splendour
    those souls who close their eyes that they may see.
And I, please, with love that goes on beyond mind
    to all that is beyond mind,
    seek to gain such for myself through this prayer.

From THE CLOUD OF UNKNOWING
    (14TH CENTURY), TRANS. ANON.

VESPERS: SATURDAY EVENING

How mighty are the Sabbaths,
  How mighty and how deep,
That the high courts of heaven
  To everlasting keep.
What peace unto the weary,
  What pride unto the strong,
When God in whom are all things
  Shall be all things to men.

Jerusalem is the city
  Of everlasting peace,
A peace that is surpassing
  And utter blessedness;
Where finds the dreamer waking
  Truth beyond dreaming far,
Nor is the heart's possessing
  Less than the heart's desire.

But of the courts of heaven
  And him who is the King,
The rest and the refreshing,
  The joy that is therein,
Let those that know it answer
  Who in that bliss have part,
If any word can utter
  The fullness of the heart.

But ours, with minds uplifted
  Unto the heights of God,
With our whole heart's desiring,
  To take the homeward road,
And the long exile over,
  Captive in Babylon,
Again unto Jerusalem,
  To win at last return.

There, all vexation ended,
  And from all grieving free,
We sing the song of Zion
  In deep security.
And everlasting praises
  For all thy gifts of grace
Rise from thy happy people,
  Lord of our blessedness.

There Sabbath unto Sabbath
   Succeeds eternally,
The joy that has no ending
   Of souls in holiday.
And never shall the rapture
   Beyond all mortal ken
Cease from the eternal chorus
   That angels sing with men.

Now to the King Eternal
   Be praise eternally,
From whom are all things, by whom
   And in whom all things be.
From whom, as from the Father,
   By whom, as by the Son,
In whom, as in the Spirit,
   Father and Son in one.

PETER ABELARD (1079–1142),   199
TRANS. HELEN WADDELL

From AMORETTI

Most glorious Lord of life! that, on this day,
Didst make thy triumph over death and sin;
And, having harrowed hell, didst bring away
Captivity thence captive, us to win:
This joyous day, dear Lord, with joy begin;
And grant that we, for whom thou didest die,
Being with thy dear blood clean washed from sin,
May live for ever in felicity!
And that thy love we weighing worthily,
May likewise love thee for the same again;
And for thy sake, that all like dear didst buy,
With love may one another entertain:
  So let us love, dear Love, like as we ought;
  Love is the lesson which the Lord us taught.

FORGIVENESS

Most merciful and loving Father,
We beseech Thee most humbly, even with all our
    hearts,
To pour out upon our enemies with bountiful hands
    whatsoever things Thou knowest may do them
    good.
And chiefly a sound and uncorrupt mind,
Where-through they may know Thee and love Thee in
    true charity and with their whole heart,
And love us, Thy children, for Thy sake.
Let not their first hating of us turn to their harm,
Seeing that we cannot do them good for want of ability.
Lord, we desire their amendment and our own.
Separate them not from us by punishing them,
But join and knot them to us by Thy favourable
    dealings with them.
And, seeing we be all ordained to be citizens of the one
    everlasting city,
Let us begin to enter into that way here already by
    mutual love,
Which may bring us right forth thither.

KEEP ME FROM SINKIN' DOWN

Oh Lord,
Oh, my Lord,
Oh, my good Lord,
Keep me from sinking down.

I tell you what I mean to do,
Keep me from sinking down,
I mean to go to heaven too;
Keep me from sinking down.

ANON., TRANSCRIBED BY ROBERT NATHANIEL
DETT (1882–1943)

LORD OF THE WORLD

Lord of the world, He reigned alone
   While yet the universe was naught.
   When by His will all things were wrought,
Then first His sovran Name was known.

And when the All shall cease to be,
   In dread lone splendour He shall reign,
   He was, He is, He shall remain
In glorious eternity.

For He is one, no second shares
   His nature or His loneliness;
   Unending and beginningless,
All strength is His, all sway He bears.

He is the living God to save,
   My Rock while sorrow's toils endure,
   My banner and my stronghold sure,
The cup of life whene'er I crave.

I place my soul within His palm
   Before I sleep as when I wake,
   And though my body I forsake,
Rest in the Lord in fearless calm.

ATTRIB. SOLOMON IBN GABRIOL (11TH CENTURY),   203
TRANS. ISRAEL ZANGWILL

I ASKED FOR STRENGTH

I asked for strength that I might achieve;
I was made weak that I might learn humbly to obey.

I asked for health that I might do greater things;
I was given infirmity that I might do better things.

I asked for riches that I might be happy;
I was given poverty that I might be wise.

I asked for power that I might have the praise of men;
I was given weakness that I might feel the need of God.

I asked for all things that I might enjoy life;
I was given life that I might enjoy all things.

I got nothing that I had asked for,
but everything that I had hoped for.

Almost despite myself my unspoken prayers were
    answered;
I am, among all men, most richly blessed.

GRACE

Lord Christ, we pray thy mercy on our table spread,
And what thy gentle hands have given thy men
Let it by thee be blessed: whate'er we have
Came from thy lavish heart and gentle hand,
And all that's good is thine, for thou art good.
And ye that eat, give thanks for it to Christ,
And let the words ye utter be only peace,
For Christ loved peace: it was himself that said,
Peace I give unto you, my peace I leave with you.
Grant that our own may be a generous hand
Breaking the bread for all poor men, sharing the food.
Christ shall receive the bread thou gavest his poor,
And shall not tarry to give thee reward.

ALCUIN OF YORK (735–804),
TRANS. HELEN WADDELL

TWO GRACES FOR CHILDREN

God! to my little meal and oil
Add but a bit of flesh, to boil:
And Thou my pipkinnet shalt see
Give a wave-offering unto Thee.

Here, a little child, I stand,
Heaving up my either hand:
Cold as paddocks though they be,
Here I lift them up to thee,
For a benison to fall
On our meat and on our all.

SHEMÀ

You who live secure
In your warm houses,
Who return at evening to find
Hot food and friendly faces:

> Consider whether this is a man,
> Who labors in the mud
> Who knows no peace
> Who fights for a crust of bread
> Who dies at a yes or a no.
> Consider whether this is a woman,
> Without hair or name
> With no more strength to remember
> Eyes empty and womb cold
> As a frog in winter.

Consider that this has been:
I commend these words to you.
Engrave them on your hearts
When you are in your house, when you walk on your way,
When you go to bed, when you rise.
Repeat them to your children.
Or may your house crumble,
Disease render you powerless,
Your offspring avert their faces from you.

PRIMO LEVI (1919–1987),
TRANS. RUTH FELDMAN AND BRIAN SWANN

THREE PETITIONS

When you sit happy in your own fair house,
   Remember all poor men that are abroad,
That Christ, who gave this roof, prepare for thee
   Eternal dwelling in the house of God.

ALCUIN OF YORK (735–804),
TRANS. HELEN WADDELL

Show love to all creatures, and thou wilt be happy; for
when thou lovest all things, thou lovest the Lord, for he
is all in all.

TULSI DAS (1532–1623)
TRANS. F. R. ALLCHIN

Have mercy on me, O Beneficent One, I was angered
    for I had no shoes:
Then I met a man who had no feet.

CHINESE SAYING,
TRANS. ANON.

AT THE DOOR OF A CHRISTIAN HOSPITAL

O God,
make the door of this house wide enough
to receive all who need human love and
fellowship, and a heavenly Father's care;
    and narrow enough to shut out
all envy, pride and hate.
    Make its threshold smooth enough
to be no stumbling-block to children,
nor to straying feet,
    but rugged enough to turn back
the tempter's power:
        make it a gateway
        to thine eternal kingdom.

THOMAS KEN (1637–1711)

COMPLINE

GUIDANCE

Lead, kindly light, amid the encircling gloom,
        Lead thou me on;
The night is dark, and I am far from home;
        Lead thou me on.
Keep thou my feet; I do not ask to see
The distant scene: one step enough for me.

I was not ever thus, nor prayed that thou
        Shouldst lead me on;
I loved to choose and see my path; but now
        Lead thou me on.
I loved the garish day, and, spite of fears,
Pride ruled my will: remember not past years.

So long thy power hath blest me, sure it still
        Will lead me on
O'er moor and fen, o'er crag and torrent, till
        The night is gone,
And with the morn those angel faces smile
Which I have loved long since, and lost awhile.

JOHN HENRY NEWMAN (1801–1890)   213

LORD, LET YOUR LIGHT BE ONLY
FOR THE DAY

Lord, let Your light be only for the day,
And the darkness for the night.
And let my dress, my poor humble dress
Lie quietly over my chair at night.

Let the church-bells be silent,
My neighbour Ivan not ring them at night.
Let the wind not waken the children
Out of their sleep at night.

Let the hen sleep on its roost, the horse in the stable
All through the night.
Remove the stone from the middle of the road
That the thief may not stumble at night.

Let heaven be quiet during the night,
Restrain the lightning, silence the thunder,
They should not frighten mothers giving birth
To their babies at night.

And me too protect against fire and water,
Protect my poor roof at night.
Let my dress, my poor humble dress
Lie quietly over my chair at night.

NECHUM BRONZE (DATE UNKNOWN), TRANS.
THE REFORM SYNAGOGUES OF GREAT BRITAIN

ALL PRAISE TO THEE, MY GOD, THIS NIGHT

All praise to Thee, my God, this night,
For all the Blessings of the Light!
Keep me, O keep me, King of kings,
Beneath Thy own Almighty Wings.

Forgive me, Lord, for Thy dear Son,
The ill that I this day have done;
That with the World, myself and Thee,
I, ere I sleep, at peace may be.

O! may my Soul on Thee repose,
And sweet sleep my Eyelids close —
Sleep, that may me more vigorous make,
To serve my God when I awake.

THOMAS KEN (1637–1711)

LORD, HEAR MY PRAYER
(*A paraphrase of Psalm 102*)

Lord, hear my prayer when trouble glooms,
Let sorrow find a way,
And when the day of trouble comes,
Turn not thy face away:
My bones like hearthstones burn away,
My life like vapoury smoke decays.

My heart is smitten like the grass,
That withered lies and dead,
And I, so lost to what I was,
Forget to eat my bread.
My voice is groaning all the day,
My bones prick through this skin of clay.

The wilderness's pelican,
The desert's lonely owl —
I am their like, a desert man
In ways as lone and foul.
As sparrows on the cottage top
I wait till I with fainting drop.

I hear my enemies reproach,
All silently I mourn;
They on my private peace encroach,
Against me they are sworn.
Ashes as bread my trouble shares,
And mix my food with weeping cares.

Yet not for them is sorrow's toil,
I fear no mortal's frowns –
But thou hast held me up awhile
And thou has cast me down.
My days like shadows waste from view,
I mourn like withered grass in dew.

But thou, Lord, shalt endure for ever,
All generations through;
Thou shalt to Zion be the giver
Of joy and mercy too.
Her very stones are in thy trust,
Thy servants reverence her dust.

Heathens shall hear and fear thy name,
All kings of earth thy glory know
When thou shalt build up Zion's fame
And live in glory there below.
He'll not despise their prayers, though mute,
But still regard the destitute.

JOHN CLARE (1793–1864)

IN THE HOUR OF MY DISTRESS

In the hour of my distress,
When temptations me oppress,
And when I my sins confess,
    Sweet Spirit comfort me!

When I lie within my bed,
Sick in heart and sick in head,
And with doubts discomforted,
    Sweet Spirit comfort me!

When the tapers now burn blue,
And the comforters are few,
And that number more than true,
    Sweet Spirit comfort me!

When the Judgment is reveal'd,
And that open'd which was seal'd,
When to Thee I have appeal'd;
    Sweet Spirit, comfort me!

LORD, WHY SHOULD I DOUBT

Lord, why should I doubt any more, when you have given me such assured pledges of your love? First, you are my creator, I your creature, you my master, I your servant. But hence arises not my comfort: you are my Father, I your child. 'You shall be my sons and daughters', says the Lord almighty. Christ is my brother: 'I ascend to my Father and your Father, to my God and your God; but, lest this should not be enough, your maker is your husband.' Nay, more, I am a member of his body, he my head. Such privileges – had not the Word of truth made them known, who or where is the man that dared in his heart have presumed to have thought it? So wonderful are these thoughts that my spirit fails in me at their consideration, and I am confounded to think that God, who has done so much for me, should have so little from me. But this is my comfort, that when I come to heaven, I shall understand perfectly what he has done for me, and then I shall be able to praise him as I ought. Lord, having this hope let me purify myself as you are pure, and let me be no more afraid of death, but even desire to be dissolved and be with you, which is best of all.

ANNE BRADSTREET (*d.* 1672)

PRAYER IN DARKNESS OF SPIRIT

O Merciful God, who answerest the poor,
   Answer us,
O Merciful God, who answerest the lowly in spirit,
   Answer us,
O Merciful God, who answerest the broken of heart,
   Answer us.
O Merciful God,
   Answer us.
O Merciful God,
   Have compassion.
O Merciful God,
   Redeem.
O Merciful God,
   Save.
O Merciful God, have pity upon us,
   Now,
   Speedily,
   And at a near time.

ABIDE WITH ME

Abide with me; fast falls the eventide;
The darkness deepens; Lord, with me abide:
When other helpers fail, and comforts flee,
Help of the helpless, oh abide with me.

Swift to its close ebbs out life's little day;
Earth's joys grow dim, its glories pass away;
Change and decay in all around I see;
O thou who changest not, abide with me.

I need thy presence every passing hour;
What but thy grace can foil the tempter's power?
Who like thyself my guide and stay can be?
Through cloud and sunshine, Lord, abide with me.

I fear no foe with thee at hand to bless;
Ills have no weight, and tears no bitterness;
Where is death's sting? where, grave, thy victory?
I triumph still, if thou abide with me.

Hold thou thy cross before my closing eyes;
Shine through the gloom, and point me to the skies;
Heaven's morning breaks, and earth's vain shadows
    flee;
In life, in death, O Lord, abide with me.

HENRY FRANCIS LYTE (1793–1847)   221

WHEN ALL WITHIN IS DARK

When all within is dark,
and former friends misprise;
from them I turn to you,
and find love in Your eyes.

When all within is dark,
and I my soul despise;
from me I turn to You,
and find love in Your eyes.

When all Your face is dark,
and Your just angers rise;
From You I turn to You,
and find love in Your eyes.

ISRAEL ABRAHAMS, BASED ON
SOLOMON IBN GABRIOL (11TH CENTURY)

SONGS OF THE SOUL IN RAPTURE AT HAVING ARRIVED AT THE HEIGHT OF PERFECTION, WHICH IS UNION WITH GOD BY THE ROAD OF SPIRITUAL NEGATION

Upon a gloomy night,
With all my cares to loving ardours flushed,
(O venture of delight!)
With nobody in sight
I went abroad when all my house was hushed.

In safety, in disguise,
In darkness up the secret stair I crept,
(O happy enterprise)
Concealed from other eyes
When all my house at length in silence slept.

Upon that lucky night
In secrecy, inscrutable to sight,
I went without discerning
And with no other light
Except for that which in my heart was burning.

It lit and led me through
More certain than the light of noonday clear
To where One waited near
Whose presence well I knew,
There where no other presence might appear.

Oh night that was my guide!
Oh darkness dearer than the morning's pride,
Oh night that joined the lover
To the beloved bride
Transfiguring them each into the other.

Within my flowering breast
Which only for himself entire I save
He sank into his rest
And all my gifts I gave
Lulled by the airs with which the cedars wave.

Over the ramparts fanned
While the fresh wind was fluttering his tresses,
With his serenest hand
My neck he wounded, and
Suspended every sense with its caresses.

Lost to myself I stayed
My face upon my lover having laid
From all endeavour ceasing:
And all my cares releasing
Threw them amongst the lilies there to fade.

ST JOHN OF THE CROSS (1542–1591),
TRANS. ROY CAMPBELL

THE NIGHT
(*John 2:3*)

    Through that pure Virgin-shrine,
That sacred veil drawn o'er thy glorious noon
That men might look and live as glow-worms shine,
        And face the moon,
    Wise Nicodemus saw such light
    As made him know his God by night.

    Most blest believer he!
Who in that land of darkness and blind eyes
Thy long expected healing wings could see
        When thou didst rise
    And, what can never more be done,
    Did at midnight speak with the sun!

    O who will tell me, where
He found thee at that dead and silent hour!
What hallowed solitary ground did bear
        So rare a flower,
    Within whose sacred leaves did lie
    The fullness of the deity?

No mercy-seat of gold,
No dead and dusty Cherub, nor carved stone,
But his own living works did my Lord hold
      And lodge alone;
    Where trees and herbs did watch and peep
    And wonder, while the Jews did sleep.

    Dear night! this world's defeat;
The stop to busy fools; care's check and curb;
The day of Spirits; my soul's calm retreat
      Which none disturb!
    Christ's progress, and his prayer time;
    The hours to which high heaven doth chime.

    God's silent, searching flight;
When my Lord's head is filled with dew, and all
His locks are wet with the clear drops of night;
      His still, soft call;
    His knocking time; the soul's dumb watch,
    When Spirits their fair kindred catch.

    Were all my loud, evil days
Calm and unhaunted as is thy dark tent,
Whose peace but by some Angel's wing or voice
      Is seldom rent;
    Then I in Heaven all the long year
    Would keep, and never wander here.

But living where the sun
Doth all things wake, and where all mix and tire
Themselves and others, I consent and run
        To every mire,
    And by this world's ill-guiding light
    Err more than I can do by night.

    There is in God, some say,
A deep, but dazzling darkness; as men here
Say it is late and dusky, because they
        See not all clear.
    O for that night! where I in him
    Might live invisible and dim.

HIS EPITAPH

Here halt, I pray you, make a little stay,
O wayfarer, to read what I have writ,
And know by my fate what thy fate shall be.
What thou art now, wayfarer, world-renowned,
I was: what I am now, so shalt thou be.
The world's delight I followed with a heart
Unsatisfied: ashes am I, and dust.

Wherefore bethink thee rather of thy soul
Than of thy flesh; – this dieth, that abides.
Dost thou make wide thy fields? in this small house
Peace holds me now: no greater house for thee.
Wouldst have thy body clothed in royal red?
The worm is hungry for that body's meat.
Even as the flowers die in a cruel wind,
Even so, O flesh, shall perish all thy pride.

Now in thy turn, wayfarer, for this song
That I have made for thee, I pray you, say:
'Lord Christ, have mercy on thy servant here,'
And may no hand disturb this sepulchre,
Until the trumpet rings from heaven's height,
'O thou that liest in the dust, arise,
The Judge of the unnumbered hosts is here!'

Alcuin was my name: learning I loved.
O thou that readest this, pray for my soul.

Here lieth the Lord Abbot Alcuin of blessed memory, who died in peace on the nineteenth of May. And when ye have read this, do ye all pray for him and say, 'May the Lord give him eternal rest.' Amen.

ALCUIN OF YORK (735–804),
        TRANS. HELEN WADDELL

NO MATTER WHERE I TURN MY HEAD

No matter where I turn my head
In village or in desert
Deep silence has engulfed the dead
And they have left no message.

Which way they disappeared, God knows,
And what has them befallen,
For I can find no news of those
Who from the cliff have fallen.

From here where do you go to stay?
What kind of dwelling is it?
Tell me, O travellers who pay
To this serai a visit.

O you who in God's favour stand
And hold the key to worship,
O blessed teachers, take my hand
And lead me to God's doorstep.

I know there is account with God
For all, that now is hidden,
Rahmān is trembling at the thought
Of what may there be written.

RAHMĀN BĀBA,
TRANS. JENS ENEVOLDSEN

THOU HAST MADE ME

Thou hast made me, and shall thy work decay?
Repair me now, for now mine end doth haste,
I run to death, and death meets me as fast,
And all my pleasures are like yesterday;
I dare not move my dim eyes any way,
Despair behind, and death before doth cast
Such terror, and my feebled flesh doth waste
By sin in it, which it t'wards hell doth weigh;
Only thou'rt above, and when towards thee
By thy leave I can look, I rise again;
But our old subtle foe so tempteth me
That not one hour my self I can sustain;
Thy Grace may wing me to prevent his art,
And thou like Adamant draw mine iron heart.

DIVINATION BY A DAFFADILL

When a Daffadill I see,
Hanging down his head t'wards me;
Guesse I may, what I must be:
First, I shall decline my head;
Secondly, I shall be dead;
Lastly, safely buryed.

ROBERT HERRICK (1591–1674)

EVEN SUCH IS TIME

Even such is Time, which takes in trust
    Our youth, our joys, and all we have,
And pays us but with age and dust:
    Who in the dark and silent grave,
When we have wandered all our ways
    Shuts up the story of our days:
And from which earth and grave and dust,
The Lord shall raise me up, I trust.

SIR WALTER RALEGH (c. 1554–1618)   233

SUBMISSION TO AFFLICTIVE PROVIDENCES
(*Job 1:21*)

Naked as from the earth we came,
    And crept to life at first,
We to the earth return again,
    And mingle with our dust.

The dear delights we here enjoy
    And fondly call our own
Are but short favours borrowed now
    To be repaid anon.

'Tis God that lifts our comforts high,
    Or sinks 'em in the grave.
He gives, and (blessed be his Name)
    He takes but what he gave.

Peace, all our angry passions then!
    Let each rebellious sigh
Be silent at his sovereign will,
    And every murmur die.

If smiling Mercy crown our lives
    Its praises shall be spread,
And we'll adore the Justice too
    That strikes our comforts dead.

BEFORE THE BEGINNING

Before the beginning Thou hast foreknown the end,
    Before the birthday the death-bed was seen of Thee:
Cleanse what I cannot cleanse, mend what I cannot
      mend.
    O Lord All-Merciful, be merciful to me.

While the end is drawing near I know not mine end:
    Birth I recall not, my death I cannot foresee:
O God, arise to defend, arise to befriend,
    O Lord All-Merciful, be merciful to me.

PRAYER

Never weather-beaten sail more willing bent to shore,
Never tired pilgrim's limbs affected slumber more,
Than my wearied sprite now longs to fly out of my
     troubled breast:
O come quickly, sweetest Lord, and take my soul to
     rest!

Ever blooming are the joys of heaven's high Paradise,
Cold age deafs not there our ears nor vapour dims our
     eyes:
Glory there the sun outshines; whose beams the
     Blessèd only see:
O come quickly, glorious Lord, and raise my sprite to
     Thee!

HYMN TO GOD THE FATHER

Wilt thou forgive that sinn where I begunn,
   Which is my sinn, though it were done before?
Wilt thou forgive those sinns, through which I runn,
   And doe them still, though still I doe deplore?
     When thou hast done, thou hast not done,
       for I have more.

Wilt thou forgive that sinn, by which I have wonne
   Others to sinn, and made my sinn their dore?
Wilt Thou forgive that sinn which I did shunne
   A yeare, or twoe, but wallowed in a score?
     When thou hast done, thou hast not done,
       for I have more.

I have a sinn of fear, that when I have spunn
   My last thred, I shall perish on the shore;
Sweare by thy selfe that at my Death thy Sunn
   Shall shine as it shines nowe, and heretofore;
     And having done that, thou hast done,
       I have noe more.

TO HIS SWEET SAVIOUR

Night hath no wings, to him that cannot sleep;
And Time seems then, not for to flie, but creep;
Slowly her chariot drives, as if that she
Had broke her wheele, or crackt her axeltree.
Just so it is with me, who list'ning, pray
The winds, to blow the tedious night away;
That I might see the cheerfull peeping day.
Sick is my heart; O Saviour! do Thou please
To make my bed soft in my sicknesses:
Lighten my candle, so that I beneath
Sleep not for ever in the vaults of death:
Let me Thy voice betimes i' th morning heare;
Call, and I'le come; say Thou, the when, and where:
Draw me, but first, and after Thee I'le run,
And make no one stop, till my race be done.

ROBERT HERRICK (1591–1674)   239

BEFORE SLEEP

The toil of day is ebbing,
    The quiet comes again,
In slumber deep relaxing
    The limbs of tired men.

And minds with anguish shaken,
    And spirits racked with grief,
The cup of all forgetting
    Have drunk and found relief.

The still Lethean waters
    Now steal through every vein,
And men no more remember
    The meaning of their pain ...

Let, let the weary body
    Lie sunk in slumber deep.
The heart shall still remember
    Christ in its very sleep.

PRUDENTIUS (4TH CENTURY),
TRANS. HELEN WADDELL

TWO PETITIONS

From the unreal lead me to the real.
From darkness lead me to light.
From death lead me to immortality.

THE UPANISHADS (800 BC)

Now may every living thing, young or old, weak or strong, living near or far, known or unknown, living or departed or yet unborn, may every living thing be full of bliss.

THE BUDDHA (*c.* 6TH CENTURY BC)

GOD BE IN MY HEAD

God be in my head
And in my understanding;
God be in myne eyes,
And in my looking;
God be in my mouth,
And in my speaking;
God be in my heart,
And in my thynking;
God be at my end,
And at my departing.

ACKNOWLEDGMENTS

Thanks are due to the following copyright holders for permission to reprint:

ALBERRY, A. J.: George Allen and Unwin, an imprint of HarperCollins *Publishers* Ltd. for an excerpt from *Sufism*, ed. A. J. Alberry. AUDEN, W. H.: Faber and Faber Ltd. and Random House, Inc. for 'Prime' by W. H. Auden from *Collected Poems*, ed. Edward Mendelson. BHAGAVAD-GĪTĀ: The Vedanta Society for an excerpt from *The Bhagavad-Gītā*, 1989, tr. Swami Prabhavananda. CAMPBELL, R.: Harvill Press Ltd. and Aitken, Stone & Wylie for translations of 'Songs of the Soul' and 'Verses written after an Ecstasy of High Exaltation' from *The Poems of St John of the Cross*. First published by Harvill, 1951. All rights reserved. HOPKINS, G. M.: © The Society of Jesus 1967 for 'My prayers must meet a brazen heaven' by Gerard Manley Hopkins. Reprinted from *The Poems of Gerard Manley Hopkins*, 1967, ed. W. H. Gardner and N. H. MacKenzie, by permission of Oxford University Press on behalf of the Society of Jesus. JARRELL, R.: Farrar, Straus & Giroux, Inc. and Faber and Faber Ltd. for 'A Prayer at Morning' by Randall Jarrell from *The Complete Poems*. © Mrs Randall Jarrell, 1969. JEWISH PRAYERS: Nechum Bronze, The Kaddish, Copyright ©

single will', 'Lord Christ, we pray thy mercy on our
table spread' and 'When you sit happy in your own fair
house' from *More Latin Lyrics* and Alcuin's 'Here halt,
I pray you, make a little stay'; Prudentius's 'The toil of
day is ebbing' and Abelard's 'How mighty are the
Sabbaths' from *Mediæval Latin Lyrics*. WEIL, S.:
International Thomson Publishing Services Ltd. for
excerpts from *Waiting for God* by Simone Weil, tr.
Emma Crauford. WOLTERS, C.: Penguin UK Ltd. for
excerpts from *The Cloud of Unknowing and Other Works*,
tr. Clifton Wolters (Penguin Classics 1961, revised
edition, 1978) copyright © Clifton Wolters, 1961,
1978.

INDEX OF FIRST LINES

Abide with me; fast falls the eventide 221

Ah, Lord, the torment of this task that Thou hast
    laid on me 113

All creatures of our God and King 147

All praise to Thee, my God, this night 215

And you may well say 'act' 36

As a fish that is dragged from the water 111

As kingfishers catch fire, dragonflies draw flame .. 129

As proud of a penny as of a pound of gold 92

Awake, my soul, and with the sun 59

Before the beginning Thou hast foreknown the
    end 236

Beloved Pan, and all ye other gods 185

Blessed by you, harsh matter, barren soil,
    stubborn rock 96

But beggars about midsummer go breadless to
    supper 88

Close mine eyes from evil 103

Cold, slow, silent, but returning, after so many
    hours 67

Creator Spirit, by whose aid 139

Dear Lord and Father of mankind 155

Dearest Lord, teach me to be generous 87

Do you seek no more of Him than to name His
    Name? 165

Elected Silence, sing to me 171
Even such is Time, which takes in trust 233
Fire of the Spirit, life of the lives of creatures 141
For ADORATION seasons change 27
Forth in thy name, O Lord, I go 68
From the unreal lead me to the real 241
Give me my scallop-shell of quiet 177
Glory be to God for dappled things 63
God be in my head 242
God give me work 122
God moves in a mysterious way 108
God strengthen me to bear myself 66
God! to my little meal and oil 206
Grant to me, O Lord, to know what I ought to
     know 103
Great and holy is the Lord 73
Great God accept our gratitude 93
Happy those early days, when I 127
Have mercy on me, O Beneficent One 208
Here halt, I pray you, make a little stay 229
How mighty are the Sabbaths 197
How should I praise thee, Lord! how should my
     rymes 24
I asked for Peace 176
I asked for strength that I might achieve 204
I caught this morning morning's minion 130
I do believe, that die I must 95

I entered in, I know not where 32
I'll hope no more 157
I moved across the Dharma-nature 189
I place before my inward eyes myself with all that
    I am 26
If at any time having cast thyself into the posture
    of prayer 38
If we human beings are mere shadows 168
In 1938 I spent ten days at Solesmes 54
In God's Name be the course and the mooring .. 80
In the hour of my distress 218
It is at those moments when we are, as we say, in a
    bad mood 104
It is glory enough for me 84
Just as the meditations of those who seek to live
    the contemplative life 19
Lead, kindly light, amid the encircling gloom 213
Leave me, O Love, which reaches but to dust 138
Let us magnify and let us sanctify the great name
    of God 195
Lord Christ, we pray thy mercy on our table
    spread 205
Lord, enfold me in the depths of your heart 137
Lord, for the erring thought 162
Lord, hear my prayer when trouble glooms 216
Lord, I have abandoned all for Thee 110
Lord Jesus Christ; Let me seek you by desiring you 100

Lord, let Your light be only for the day 214
Lord, make me an instrument of Thy peace 90
Lord, not for light in darkness do we pray 85
Lord of fire and death, of wind and moon and waters 71
Lord of the world, He reigned alone 203
Lord, teach me to seek Thee 42
Lord, why should I doubt any more 219
Love bade me welcome; yet my soul drew back . .. 56
Make us worthy, Lord 87
May there be peace in the higher regions 180
Most glorious Lord of life! that, on this day 200
Most merciful and loving Father 201
My own heart let me more have pity on; let 193
My period had come for Prayer 43
My prayers must meet a brazen heaven 142
My soul, there is a country 183
My spirit longs for Thee 143
Naked as from the earth we came 234
Never weather-beaten sail more willing bent to
        shore 237
Nevertheless, there are helps which the
        apprentice in contemplation should employ .. 152
New every morning is the love 65
Night hath no wings, to him that cannot sleep 239
No deeds I've done nor thoughts I've thought 114
No matter where I turn my head 231
Not to serve the foolish, but to serve the wise 163

Now may every living thing 241
O God, early in the morning I cry to you 64
O God, make the door of this house wide enough 209
O Lord God, when Thou givest to Thy servants
    to endeavour 122
O Lord, in Mercy grant my soul to live 80
O Merciful God, who answerest the poor 220
O most high, almighty, good Lord God 131
O thou who camest from above 102
Of what avail this restless, hurrying activity? 112
Oh Lord, Oh my Lord 202
One goodness ruleth by its single will 167
One great Discouragement to Felicity 173
One hundred feet from off the ground 107
Praise be to him who alone is to be praised 144
Praise to the Holiest in the height 44
Prayer is the little implement 18
Prayer, the Church's banquet, Angels' age 17
Prayer unites the soul to God 18
Retirèd thoughts enjoy their own delights 181
Set Love in order, thou that lovest Me 101
Show love to all creatures 208
Simultaneously, as soundlessly 69
Since Lov will thrust in it self as the Greatest of
    all Principles 51
Summer ends now; now, barbarous in beauty, the
    stooks rise 190

Sweet Peace, where dost thou dwell? I humbly
    crave 178
Take Lord, unto Thyself 113
The afternoon had been stormy 191
The Church is the house of prayer 46
The Corn was Orient and Immortal Wheat 125
The Moon's the same old moon 189
The Perfect Way is only difficult for those who
    pick and choose 91
The sleepless Hours who watch me as I lie 134
The soul that is faithful in the exercise of love 158
The toil of day is ebbing 240
The view from my bedroom window looking up
    the dingle 61
The whole virtue of religious practices 28
The world is charged with the grandeur of God .. 97
The world's bright comforter, whose beamsome
    light 136
There are three different paths to reach the
    Highest 185
There are two ways of introducing a soul into
    prayer 29
There comes an hour when begging stops 39
There is a light that shines beyond all things on
    earth 133
There was a roaring in the wind all night 115
They are all gone into the world of light! 145

Thou hast made me, and shall thy work decay? .. 232
Thou shalt have one God only; who 94
Though our mouths were full of song as the sea .. 72
Through that pure Virgin-shrine 226
Thy kingdom come. That is, may your reign be
    realised here 98
To Mercy Pity Peace and Love 50
Upon a gloomy night 223
What is more Easy and Sweet then Meditation? .. 151
What various hindrances we meet 40
When a Daffadill I see 233
When all within is dark 222
When first my lines of heav'nly joys made mention 49
When I consider how my light is spent 84
When the heart is hard and parched up 194
When Thou dost take 35
When you sit happy in your own fair house 208
Wherever I went I met words and did not
    understand them 184
Who says that fictions only and false hair 48
Who would true Valour see 83
Why dost Thou shade Thy lovely face? O why .. 78
Wilt thou forgive that sinn where I begunn 238
Wonderful to come out living 137
You are wisdom, uncreated and eternal 196
You that have spent the silent night 74
You who live secure 207